FEATURING
FLORIDA

FEATURING FLORIDA

FLORIDA

The Sunshine State in Fiction, Film & TV

CAREN SCHNUR NEILE

THE
History
PRESS

Published by The History Press
Charleston, SC
www.historypress.com

Cover image: *AllStar Picture Library Limited/Alamy Stock Photo*.

First published 2025

Manufactured in the United States

ISBN 9781467155809

Library of Congress Control Number: 2024947364

For Miles, Kai and Gibson, beautiful boys all.

Because this is Florida, we can be what we choose to be.

—*Campbell McGrath*

Contents

CONTENTS

CONTENTS

Acknowledgments

M any thanks to my dear friend Jennifer Bourdain, who helped birth this book.

Thank you, Joe Gartrell, for believing in this project from the start.

Thank you to the ever-helpful staff of the Boca Raton Public Library, particularly Sheryl Bish, whose display of Florida-based holdings quite possibly saved my life and definitely saved this project.

Thanks also to the supportive residents of Verena at Delray and The Forum at Deer Creek in Deerfield Beach, who patiently listened to and commented on early versions of this work.

Thank you to the wonderful Florida Humanities, which has allowed me to travel the state testing out this material.

Thank you to Rodney Welch, Florida expert extraordinaire, for your invaluable fact-checking.

Thank you to the prodigiously talented Campbell McGrath for your kind permission to quote from your gorgeous poetry.

Thanks always to Tom, for everything I do and for everything you do.

Introduction

They *Are* Making This Up!

*If they had any sense
of history
it would be called Landgrab…
it would be called Exploitationia…
—Campbell McGrath*

I thought more than once that I would never finish writing this book. Oh, it had all seemed so fun and simple in the planning stages! Just watch a slew of Florida-themed movies and TV shows and read a lot of fiction that was not only set in Florida but also set in Florida for a reason. How hard could it be? I figured that maybe these would total about fifty in all. What, I intended to discover, did these creative endeavors have to say about places and topics like the iconic Space Coast? Or the changing waves of crime, for that matter? The Cuban exiles? The pioneer days? The environmental, economic and cultural impact of Disney World and both civic-minded and rapacious developers? The revolution in cosmetic surgery?

Then I started to watch. And read. And sweat—not solely because I was working in a subtropical climate, although, frankly, that always comes into play down here—but also because the more Florida fare I uncovered in my research, the more I realized there was to consume. Not only the classic classics, like Rawlings's *The Yearling*, Hurston's *Their Eyes Were Watching God* or Hemingway's *To Have and Have Not*. Or the newer classics, by writers like Hiaasen, Buchanan and MacDonald. There were also the relative newcomers to the state's literature, written by people with impressive literary reputations elsewhere, such as Michener, Leonard and Grisham. Then there were the equally absorbing and revealing even newer films and books by less well-known creatives, like *The Florida Project* (Baker) and *Florida Woman* (Rogers). *And what to do about all that TV?* Not to mention a few short story collections. It seems that for quite some time now, everyone has wanted to set a story in Florida. Not that I can blame them. There is a lot to write about here. But where, I asked myself, was it all going to end?

One thing I didn't ask myself was *why* I was doing it. Above all, I wanted to make the case that although it's safe to assume that most Americans think of Miami as a whole lot less cultured than, say, New York or Los Angeles, we do have our share of fine literature, not only in that city but also throughout this magnificent state. We also have novel-writing boat captains and English professors. Besides them, heavy hitters from outside the state are intrigued enough to hang around for a while. In short, Florida has something to say, and others have something to say about Florida.

There's more to the answer, of course. The beloved Miami author and columnist Dave Barry has a catchphrase when he's writing nonfiction about Florida craziness: "I am not making this up!" When it comes to the Sunbaked State, there certainly is enough absurd reality to go around without having to resort to fiction. So, why write about Florida *fiction* when every other local news item reveals another real-life crazy Florida man?

In fact, I recently heard an interview with a non-Floridian, non-American, non-creative that answered that question perfectly. Justin Trudeau, the prime minister of Canada and son of another, was asked in an interview about why he read and advocated for the reading of fiction. "Getting kids to read stories," he said, "is sometimes one of the first ways they discover empathy. Because you have to see yourself in the main character to get any enjoyment out of the book. And being aware of how someone thinks and feels about anything is a complete opening of the world." If I had been interviewing him, I would have asked if it isn't also a pleasure. Plus, I would have thanked him for the plug for fiction.

As a storyteller and both a student and teacher of storytelling and literature, I have come to believe that the story is the single most effective rhetorical tool that humans possess, appealing as it does first and foremost to emotion but also reflecting to a lesser extent both logic and community norms. I have long studied how culture, personality and experience are woven together in fictional narrative, how the ethos of a group and a place is borne on the wings of a well-told tale.

Quite simply, when we are immersed in the life of a fictional character, we come to know that person—if they are written well—like we know no one but ourselves. We often know their innermost thoughts and secrets. We also see their environment through their eyes. We feel as though we were living in their time. We begin to understand things about humans and their habitats that we could never quite understand as well otherwise. What's more, we see that we are not alone.

There is a time and a place for facts, for truth with a lowercase *t*. Works of history depend on them. So does journalism. So, in fact, do our relationships. But art can do something that other media cannot. Art can show us Truth with a capital *T*, the Truth of human experience. It can help us realize the subjunctive, the what-if of life in general and of our lives in particular. If we exercise our imaginations through art, we can imagine all sorts of possibilities and alternatives in our own lives. And that's good—as long, of course, as we're clear about the distinction between fact and fiction.

Art can also be a delight. So, as much reading and viewing as I've done over the past year—there are ninety entries here—I've also done my share of delighting in it. I hope this book inspires you to do so, too.

WHAT MAKES A FLORIDA STORY?

The late Israeli folklorist Dov Noy once said that the four characteristics that make up Jewish stories are: Jewish people, place, time and/or ethics. The same can be said of a Florida story,

First, let's look at the connection between Florida people and Florida place. Local author Lauren Groff believes that the environment has a lot to do with the characters that people Florida literature, and I think she has a point. When hurricane-force winds have long been a part of Florida life; when a heat so searing and pervasive that, on leaving an airport after some time away, you recognize the feel of moist gauze swaddling your body; when alligators swallow children who play too close to man-made lakes built on developments in the Everglades, the adrenaline starts to rise. We feel stressed and worried. Add to that a fast-and-lose frontier environment that has never been completely civilized, and you've got trouble in the human environment as well. Folks get wary. City dwellers learn to be wary anywhere; rural types are wary of city dwellers, and everyone is wary of the tourists.

Anyone discussing Florida must mention the notorious Florida man meme, and I do discuss several works that are, in one way or another, based on it. This meme suggests that Floridians, our young men in particular, are ignorant lawbreakers who can't help getting caught red-handed in poorly thought-out schemes. Hey, give us a break. It's a big state with a lot of people. And it gets hot. People often drink a lot of beer and drinks with paper parasols, and they often have time on their hands. And yes, our educational system is not always the best. Is "Florida man" what you choose to believe about us? I tend to think we're the butt of jokes because, as pioneers, we are eager to try new things, some of them unfortunately involving the use of heavy machinery when inebriated. But I'm also willing to bet there are plenty of "New York men," "Texas men" and "California men" as well. In any case, I don't know too many Floridians who are overly embarrassed by the expression. Some of us are even undoubtedly proud.

Then, of course, there are the immigrants, whether they are internally displaced from other regions of the country or from overseas. Florida has the second-largest concentration of non-natives in the country, which explains the spate of "Florida native" bumper stickers out there. This is particularly true in the southern part of the state. Younger people tend to have been born here; on the southeast coast, the older residents are often from the New York metropolitan area or else from Canada, the Caribbean and Central and South America. In the southwest, many of the immigrants are from the Midwest. And don't forget that Tarpon Springs owes its rich culture to people of Greek heritage, whose immigration to the region dates to the late nineteenth century.

Florida time is also wrapped up in the idea of place. While out-of-staters sometimes think we have no seasons, we definitely have hurricane season, traditionally from June 1 to November 30, although, these days, it's threatening to lengthen by a few weeks or more. We used to have more of an actual winter—those places that managed to evade it have names like Frostproof and Miami—but whether or not the weather changes much anymore, we do have a winter season, when the tourists come to play and cultural events from concerts to festivals appear in full force. Almost everything slows down in summer, even though the advent of air-conditioning in the 1950s changed the state forever, particularly the southernmost outposts. In addition, the time from about March to August along the state's southern Atlantic coast is sea lice season (actually tiny crustaceans), when ocean bathers must be particularly careful to rinse after swimming to avoid itchy rashes.

As for Florida ethics, there is definitely a Margaritaville live-and-let-live vibe to much of Florida life, particularly in the south, most specifically in the Keys, where it got its name. The farther north you roam, the more like the American South the state is, with more conservative politics and attitudes, except, perhaps, among the college students, who may come from anywhere. Hey, at more than sixty-five thousand square miles and 23 million residents, we've got a lot of diversity. Still, many of us realize that we are living on the edge, in one way or another. The edge of the nation. The edge of existence. In flat-as-a-pancake South Florida, for example, the combination of overflowing lakes and rivers with water seeping up from porous limestone may well overtake us before too many decades have passed. Yet we stay, and folks keep on moving down to get their own slice of paradise before it disappears. The attitude to our changing environment often seems to come from our laid-back Spanish speakers: *Mañana*!

WHAT THIS BOOK IS—AND WHAT IT IS NOT

So, this book is a celebration of artists' renditions of Florida and Floridians on video and film, as well as in print, ranging from 1887 (*The Flamingo Feather*, which is still available) to early 2024 (*Bad Boys: Ride or Die* and *Palm Royale*). It is also a look behind the characters and their stories, giving some context to, say, the Mariel Boatlift that brought over the likes of Tony Montana (*Scarface*) and the multiple members of multiple families named Perez (*The Perez Family*). Wrecker culture (*Dark Light*), the importance of oranges to the state's economy and self-image (*Goldens Are Here*) and the promise and pitfalls that accompanied the expansion of Major League Baseball to Miami (*Done Deal*) are also highlighted, not to mention the changing face of aspects of life such as retirement (*Cocoon* and *Recessional*), the environment (*Under Cover of Daylight*) and crime (*Orchid Beach*, the Bad Boys franchise, *Cold Florida* and much, much more). Readers will find some behind-the-scenes information about movie casts, directors and authors, awards and trivia, particularly in the "fun facts" sections that accompany many of the entries.

What this book is *not* is just as important. Sadly, it is not, and cannot possibly be, a comprehensive guide to every single fictional representation of Florida, particularly when a single author has written many such books— and when others are being written and films and TV shows are being shot as we speak. I couldn't include the entire oeuvre of iconic Miami writer

Carl Hiaasen, for example, including the 2024 series *Bad Monkey*, based on his novel. (He's already represented more than a few times because not only did he write the novel *Star Island*, but he also wrote the book for the movie *Hoot*, and he contributed to the group novel *Naked Came the Manatee*. What could I do?) The same goes for Edna Buchanan, Tim Dorsey, James Hall, Patrick D. Smith—even the household name John Grisham wrote more than one Florida novel. I did not include *The Whistler*, for example, although I did refer jointly to his entire Camino series. And speaking of *Hoot*, I steered away from stories written exclusively for young people and focused instead on the family movies made from those books. I also was unable to include self-published fiction, as well as stories in literary journals that did not make it into collections, although many of them are well worth reading.

Among those books and movies I regret I did not get to write about in full:

Paula Marantz Cohen's *Jane Austen in Boca* (2000), which the venerable *Kirkus Reviews* dubs "a silly trifle, but clever and fun," is the amusing tale of how three seventy-something Jewish retirees, transplanted like so many others from the Northeast to tony Boca Raton, navigate life and love. The novel is not only a tribute to the beloved nineteenth-century author's oeuvre, particularly *Pride and Prejudice*, but it is also social commentary in its own right. More than one Boca resident will thrill to the mention of another Northeast transplant, the shopping mecca Loehmann's.

Boca Daze (2012), by Steven M. Forman, features Eddie Perlmutter, a retired cop from Boston who, as the principal of the Boca Knights Detective Agency, encounters in the city, among unfortunate stereotypes like "Boca Babes, retired usetabees and Early Bird Specials" (as the flyleaf reports), more than his share of skinheads, Russian mobsters and, you guessed it, a late-in-life love affair. A previous installment in the mystery series, which incidentally has some important things to say about gay rights, healthcare and antisemitism, among other issues, has been compared to the work of the late, great Elmore Leonard on amphetamines.

Heart of Palm (2013), the first novel of Laura Lee Smith, is the saga of well-bred Arla Bolton of St. Augustine, who was said to have married beneath her when she hooked up with Dean Bravo of fictional Utina, a town that was, shall we say, not known for its country clubs and debutante balls. Suffice it to say, the marriage had its challenges, helping make the book's depiction of small-town life stack up favorably to the work of heavyweights like Fannie Flagg and Richard Russo.

Barb and Star Go to Vista Del Mar (2021) is a light-as-air romp from Kristen Wiig and Annie Mumolo (of *Bridesmaids* fame), who cowrote and star in the film. They play less-than-brilliant best friends who, on finding themselves fired (with cause) from their jobs selling furniture in the cold of Soft Rock, Nebraska, head to the fictional town of Vista Del Mar, where they encounter all manner of challenges (think villains, henchmen, mosquitoes and banana rides) under the blazing sun. Think of it as the theatrical equivalent of a silly beach read.

Blood in the Cut (2024), by Alejandro Nodarse, is a Miami neo-noir par excellence set in and around Little Havana, and it features an ex-con named Iggy Guerra who returns from a three-year prison stint to his family home and butcher shop with unforgettable repercussions—for both human and non-human animals alike. The intensity begins like a fist grabbing your collar with the heartbreaking father-son relationship, and it never lets you go. Beware of sharp objects.

NOTEWORTHY

I wrote about very few things that I actively disliked, and in all cases, I thought there was something worthwhile to glean from exploring these works. I also didn't write thumbs-up or thumbs-down reviews. If something was a big hit, I usually mentioned it. If it spawned sequels, I brought that up. That said, I did have some favorites, as well as some big surprises.

First, I am here to report that, no big surprise here, the four classic authors associated with Florida—none of whom were native to the state, incidentally—do, at least in my opinion, more than earn their sterling reputations. I heartily urge you to discover for yourselves how Marjorie Kinnan Rawlings, Marjory Stoneman Douglas, Zora Neale Hurston and Ernest Hemingway all contributed stunning, important works of fiction to the state's literary archives, with, respectively, *The Yearling*, *A River in Flood*, *Their Eyes Were Watching God* and *To Have and Have Not*. Plus, I flat-out adored the quirky *Cold Florida*. I also wholeheartedly recommend two relative newcomers to Florida art: the films *Ulee's Gold* and, although it was even more difficult to watch, *The Florida Project*. I am also proud to declare that I was one of the many who rued the day that *Bloodline* was canceled.

There were also some unexpected gifts. You could have knocked me over with a flamingo feather, for example, when I sat down to watch *Where the Boys Are*. Fully prepared to breeze through a joke of a movie, I was quite interested to find a pretty serious take on spring break and on young women's approach to the sexual revolution in the 1960s. (I admit, it was also fun to see a crazy young George Hamilton.) And although I am not generally a fan of the kinds of thrillers you can read on the beach in two days, more than one of those I read for this book kept me up way past my bedtime.

HOUSEKEEPING

I originally intended to organize the entries according to the geography of the state, but sadly, the vast majority of Florida stories are written about the southern, especially the southeastern, coast. Then I was thinking of setting the movies, novels, TV shows and story collections apart—but so many of the entries overlapped genres that that plan soon fell apart. Instead, the book is organized alphabetically to make it easy for readers to find familiar titles and browse others. In writing the individual entries, moreover, I have made every effort to keep in mind what topic in the work is most meaningful to the Florida scene. If two or more entries engage with the same topic, I try not to repeat too much background information and instead stress what that particular work brings to its audience.

As for photographs, film and TV are visual media. I've made every effort, with the resources available to me, to represent as many shows as possible through photographs. In the case of written fiction, I represented the text either with an author photograph or with a nod to the subject matter involved. The movies and TV shows were a lot easier to depict, of course, and a lot more fun as well.

SO, WHAT DOES IT ALL MEAN?

There is a common denominator to most of the stories I discuss here. To a great extent, a conflict and crisis of some sort is present in virtually every piece of dramatic art. The path toward the resolution of that conflict is what makes both the story and the characters come alive. That said, I do think that there is an undercurrent of danger to most of our Florida stories. You see it in the police procedurals and the mysteries, sure. But you also find it in *Cross Creek*, *Back to Blood*, *Florida Woman* and *Goldens Are Here*, to name just a few. These works of art tell us that whether we're on a street in downtown

Miami, underwater in the Gulf or in an orange grove in the state's central east coast, we face danger from weather, water, animals and, above all, humans. After spending forty years in the state, I would say that the risks are worth it. If you don't know it already from experience, you'll soon find that there is simply no place like Florida. And as several of these works express, from *The Deep Blue Good-by* to *Under Cover of Daylight* and beyond, it's not going to last forever. The cracks are showing through the façade wherever we look. We must do what we can to save this remarkable place, but we must also do what we can to enjoy it.

You know, I can't say I'm as thrilled to have completed this book as I thought I'd be. It's been an amazing ride. And it's been an honor to showcase Florida fiction.

100% Pure Florida Fiction: An Anthology (2000)

Edited by Susan Hubbard and Robley Wilson

NOSTALGIA AND LOSS

When two English professors from Orlando and Iowa set about to create an anthology of Florida short stories, how did they choose their material? The twenty-one stories in *100% Pure Florida Fiction* represent a good cross-section of genders, locations, ethnicities and classes. They feature a wide range of subject matter, including homophobia, loyalty, child abuse, hauntings and, because they are about the human condition, prodigious helpings of love and death. Their contributors range from writing program graduates to local university professors and more than a few major players in nationally and internationally acclaimed fiction, including Abraham Verghese, Frederick Barthelme, Alison Lurie, Jill McCorkle and Joy Williams. Most importantly, like the volume you are currently reading, the stories may not be said to be able to occur *only* in the state, but they certainly reflect themes, subjects and personalities that feel exactly right for a Florida locale.

It's a truism in a certain kind of good fiction: the place is not only a setting but also a character. And indeed, the flora and fauna, weather and characters in this collection have the feel of post-1985 Florida, which was the editors' mandate. The condos, strip malls and theme parks here are part of the landscape as they are elsewhere, but as the editors note, the sense of nostalgia and loss, of a paradise gone or a paradise that never was, is everywhere.

One of the most darkly humorous stories is a case in point. "Critterworld" is the tale of a one-hundred-year-old elephant whose final days consist of a hellish gig chained to the gate of a down-at-the-heels theme park that the narrator considers the saddest place in the state, perhaps the entire country. When the elephant suddenly drops dead, the park owner wants to preserve and stuff him, as, suddenly, he believes the creature deserves to be handled with care. The townspeople, however, have other ideas. They hack the tail and tusks and other pieces off the poor beast's corpse, partly in an effort to make removal easier and partly in the spirit of souvenir hunting. Or is there something else going on as well? Something more metaphorical?

In a marvelous set-up, the narrator explains that the elephant's name was not Stash, as in *trash*, but it was Stash, as in *lost*. What? The strangeness of the insights and images mount, as a group of gifted eighth-graders witness the scene from on top of a Volkswagen, with a screaming child inside. (The parents parked the car so close because when they arrived, they believed the elephant was already dead.) The indignity of the life, death and dismemberment of a magnificent animal not even indigenous to the area, which occurred at yet another cheesy roadside tourist attraction, is emblematic of the tackiness that takes up a fair amount of the state's legacy.

There is, however, hope. The story's young narrator's sensitivity reminds us that we can and will do better.

Adaptation (2002)

Film Directed by Spike Jonze; Starring Nicolas Cage, Meryl Streep, Chris Cooper and John Cusack

FLORIDA FLORA

It's fiction. It's nonfiction. It's an adaptation of a book. It's wildly original. It's a thriller. It's a comedy. It's about writer's block. It's about obsession. Screenwriter Charlie Kaufman's tour de force mash-up movie is as wonderful, strange and rare as the ghost orchid (also known as the palm polly or white frog orchid) it features. It is, in fact, such an elegant mélange of nature and nonsense that it could only have been set in one of the plant's few natural habitats: the Fakahatchee Strand Preserve National Park in the wholly unique Florida Everglades.

More than a few Floridians are a little obsessed with these elegant members of the *Orchidaceae* family of plants. Orchids, long a symbol of sexuality and used in modern medicine for this purpose, are known for their leaves with parallel veins; large, colorful flowers that emit a powerful scent; and their unique-among-the-plant-world bisexuality. They can also be flat-out gorgeous.

The award-winning film version of *The Orchid Thief*—Chris Cooper, for one, earned an Academy Award for Best Supporting Actor for playing the thief— is at least as loopy as Kaufman's debut feature, *Being John Malkovich*. It's also as offbeat as *New Yorker* writer Susan Orleans's nonfiction book by the same name, although in a totally different way. In *Adaptation*, fictional Kaufman (played by the redoubtable Nicolas Cage) experiences crippling writer's block because he can't figure out a way to put Orleans's supposedly unfilmable book on film. Enter Kaufman's nonexistent twin brother (also Cage), the orchid thief from the book, a wholly made-up affair between Orleans and the orchid thief, and an equally fictional attempt from the lovers to kill Kaufman. And I haven't even mentioned the sequence about the origin of life on Earth. The great Italian surrealist filmmaker Federico Fellini, who cowrote and directed a movie about not being able to make a movie, would have been proud.

Orchids belong to the *Orchidaceae* family of plants. *Wikimedia Commons.*

Actually, in this case, art imitated life. Although he lacks a twin brother, Kaufman really did experience writer's block when he realized how tough the book would be to present as a straightforward film. He took a giant gamble in writing this bizarre screenplay, and it paid off big. He's not the only person to find that to be the case in this miraculous state. Not by a long shot.

FUN FACTS ABOUT *ADAPTATION*

The screenplay was credited to not only Charlie Kaufman but also his fictional twin brother, Donald, who, although he does not exist, was thus nominated for an Academy Award. Also, the real orchid thief, horticulturist John Laroche, actually claimed, in his defense, that he was innocent due to a provision in the law against harvesting orchids that exempted members of the Seminole tribe, for whom he worked. According to his defense, he only did what he did in an effort to have the loophole closed (also to make a fortune for the Seminoles and himself by cloning the plants by the millions, thereby making them so ubiquitous that he would be saving them in their wild state). The plan failed, and he was convicted. Now, only about two thousand ghost orchids exist in the state.

All the Water I've Seen Is Running (2021)

Novel by Elias Rodriques

YOU CAN GO HOME AGAIN

Palm Coast is part of the Deltona-Daytona-Ormond Beach metropolitan area, twenty-five miles south of St. Augustine. Before its development in the late 1960s, it was known for good hunting and fishing in the pine forest, swampland and beyond. There was also a turpentine distillery (making commercial use of the pine trees), a few beach houses and farms and a small business district.

For Daniel, Rodriques's mixed-race Jamaican-born narrator in post-2008 America, it may not be much, but it's home. Never mind that he grew up Black in a racially biased community that lies between where—as he suggests early on—Trayvon Martin was shot for no reason in Sanford and Marissa Alexander was arrested for self-defense in Jacksonville. It makes no difference that he is gay in a largely homophobic neighborhood. Or that he ran track and overachieved in school so he could win a college scholarship and get out of town. Or that he left as soon as he graduated high school for California and then New York City. This is where his friends are, Black and white, male and female, track teammates and others. This is who he is. So, why did it take him seven years to return?

Only the news of the death of Daniel's best friend from high school, a wild white girl named Aubrey, brings him back home to his northern Florida roots. This few-day visit, related in dreamy, almost impressionistic prose, is a trip to the time, space and people Daniel had intended to leave behind for good. In memory after memory, whether through his storytelling sessions with old friends, his own reminiscences of family stories or his dreams, the young man reconnects with his Jamaican ancestors, his own childhood, old hip hop music and the ocean, river and roads that he realizes still course through his veins.

Will Daniel move back to Palm Coast, as he suggests in an alcohol-fueled burst of nostalgia? It hardly matters. Florida, with all its dangers, humiliations and joys, has moved back to him.

FUN FACT ABOUT
ALL THE WATER I'VE SEEN IS RUNNING

The fact that author Elias Rodriques teaches African American literature at Sarah Lawrence College in Bronxville, New York, may be a clue about what his hero decides to do after his visit back home.

The Apartment (2023)

Novel by Ana Menéndez

TO LET

From 1942 to 2012, apartment 2B in the fictional Art Deco–style apartment building known as The Helena on South Miami Beach plays host to a diverse cast of tenants, including people of Anglo-American, Asian and Latin American descent, people in love and otherwise happy families. Each chronological chapter is a self-contained story with its own period and characters; indeed, excerpts appeared in a number of publications before the book came out.

It's no coincidence that the building is designed in the Art Deco style. Characterized by pops of pastels and bright colors, geometric lines and curves, distinctive window trims and chrome accents, Art Deco was popular in the 1920s and 1930s, when Miami Beach was growing. Architects like Murray Dixon and Albert Anis left their imprints on the area that now features more of the style than any other place in the nation. The Art Deco Historic District spans along Collins Avenue, Ocean Drive and Washington Avenue, from Fifth to Twenty-Third Streets. To tour the area is to take several steps back in time.

Time, in fact, is as important to *The Apartment* as the space in which the novel is set, because no tenant lives in the same 2B as those who inhabited it before. The book is about the changing face of Miami Beach, indeed of all of Florida. It actually opens in a brief prologue set not in 1942, but rather nearly four hundred years earlier, a season or so before the Spanish conquistador Pedro Menéndez de Avilés put his mark on St. Augustine, three hundred miles away, in 1565. This was just before everything changed for the first time.

Over the seventy years that we see 2B, it is spruced up and then eventually left to deteriorate. Meanwhile, the surrounding area endures a German U-boat off Cape Canaveral, a 1952 coup in Cuba, a revolution in the same country in 1959, the growth of a mainland Miami neighborhood dubbed Little Havana and hotels and restaurants coming, going and simply being reimagined. We read along with a tenant to discover that the Collins of Collins Avenue was a real person: John Collins, who planted avocados. We learn about Carl Fisher of Fisher Island, who used a mechanical plow to harvest the mangroves. We find that Miami Beach rose from the swampland habitat of rabbits and crocodiles thanks to the crazy sales tactics of developers, the dredging and rerouting of water, nature's own successful redevelopment in the form of fierce hurricanes and jobs and apartments available only to the right sort of people.

Through it all, death looms just out of sight, because decay is as necessary as birth in an ever-changing landscape. We witness, we pay tribute and we move on.

FUN FACT ABOUT *THE APARTMENT*

According to author Ana Menéndez, the book took her a decade to write.

Apples Never Fall (2021)

Novel by Liane Moriarty

Apples Never Fall (2024)

TV Series Starring Annette Bening, Sam Neill, Alison Brie, Jake Lacy and Georgia Flood

TENNIS, ANYONE?

Once upon a time, people—mostly men—in Florida who had a little money and desired to be both active and social took up golf. They still do, of course. But then, with the growing popularity of professional tennis and the improving physical fitness of many amateur athletes, tennis exploded. Today, you need every one of your fingers and toes to count the number of tennis schools in South Florida alone, starting with the Evert Academy, the establishment of the formerly no. 1 ranked player Chris Evert, who was born in nearby Fort Lauderdale. What's more, virtually every fancy gated community and township features its share of tennis courts.

Moriarty's mystery centers around Joy, a former tennis star who, with her husband, Stan, has just retired and sold their own tennis academy in West Palm Beach. Maybe the couple should have taken up beekeeping or done some volunteer work. Instead, they have too much time on their hands, so when a mysterious young woman who calls herself Savannah rings their doorbell in crisis, Joy, in particular, bonds with her and serves as a surrogate mother. Eight months later, Joy disappears. The story, told in the present and in flashbacks to the six weeks when Savannah stayed with the couple, explains how it is that all four of the couple's grown children become more or less convinced (depending on how their father treated them when they were younger) that not only is their mother dead, but it was their father who killed her.

Meanwhile we see a lot of blue skies and palm trees, a little tennis and a wholly believable hurricane for which, for some reason, this family, who has presumably weathered dozens of storms, is strangely

Tennis plays a pivotal role in *Apples Never Fall. Wikimedia Commons.*

unprepared for. (Sure, they were facing a catastrophe, but they didn't even take in the chairs!)

Recently, many of those tennis courts in gated communities and local parks have been converted for pickleball. The sport is said to be a lot easier on the joints for older people who used to play tennis. So, stay tuned for the first pickleball thriller. You heard it here first.

FUN FACT ABOUT *APPLES NEVER FALL*

In the series, Annette Bening plays the mother of four children, and she repeatedly complains that she gets no help from them. She is the mother of four in real life, as well, and she is the youngest of four. As of this writing, we've heard no complaints.

Aquamarine (2006)

Film Directed by Elizabeth Allen Rosenbaum; Starring Emma Roberts, Sara Paxton, Jake McDorman, JoJo Levesque and Arielle Kebbel

BFFs

"There's something very fishy about that girl."

In this crazy *"Mean Girls* meets *Splash"* comedy set in a small town near Tampa, a character utters that memorable line to describe a teenaged mermaid who must find love even faster than her teenaged human girlfriends in order to prevent her father from going ahead with an arranged marriage for her back under the sea. (Hey, we don't make the rules. We just report them.) That's the "ticking clock" that propels the action in this pratfall-filled American-Australian production about young women who intend to control their own fate. Yeah, it's a fantasy, all right.

Violent storms bring up all kinds of things from the ocean floor, and one of them unearths Aquamarine, a blonde beauty with a tail that comes out only when she's wet or the sun is down. The storm in question is apparently a response from above to desperate prayers by two best friends who don't want to be separated when the mother of one of them, a marine biologist, must relocate to Australia. Unfortunately, Aquamarine's first crush is on the one boy (Wouldn't you know?) the girls have had their eyes on for years. They are unwilling to help her learn how to catch the guy until she promises to grant them a wish. ("I thought only genies granted wishes!" one of them exclaims. To which the mermaid replies scornfully, "You believe in genies?") The wish, of course, is to keep them together. For that, they'll even give up the cute lifeguard.

A mermaid entertains visitors at Seaquest Aquarium in Royal Palm Beach. *Wikimedia Commons.*

Yes, it's that kind of movie. But the whole mermaid thing really is important to Florida. While the first mention of a mermaid was in fact believed to be a Babylon god from the fourth century BCE, none other than Christopher Columbus believed he sighted one in 1492. Actually, what he encountered was most likely a manatee, otherwise known as a sea cow. Manatees are herbivorous marine mammals that live in Florida waters, as well as those of the Caribbean and Africa, and they can grow to up to fourteen feet in length and weigh as much as a ton. They are so fervently protected down here that there are actually "manatee zones" where boats are cautioned to go slowly— under penalty of a sizable fine—in order to prevent harm or harassment to the creatures. So many pirates, explorers and others have mistaken them for mermaids, in fact, that the scientific name for manatees is *Sirenia*, a callback to the alluring sirens of Greek myth.

Not that anyone is willing to admit that mermaids don't exist. After a tongue-in-cheek "documentary" about mermaids aired by Animal Planet in 2013, the National Oceanic and Atmospheric Administration was overrun with callers demanding to know the truth about the mythical beings. To which they replied: "There is no truth about mermaids."

And yet. The mermaid narrative, enhanced by Hans Christian Andersen and the Disney version of his story, lives on, even feted in Coney Island, New York, with an annual parade. To cash in on the interest, Weeki Wachee Springs State Park in Spring Hill has been luring tourists with live mermaid shows since 1947. They even eat and drink down there, although I'm not sure why they'd want to. I mean, everybody knows they can come on land as long as they dry their legs or the sun is out. Am I right?

Why do little girls in particular love mermaids so much? Perhaps it's the fact that they're usually female. (Mermen are occasionally mentioned, yeah, but nah.) They are also always beautiful. Seriously, have you ever seen a less-than-gorgeous mermaid? Or perhaps it's because they live the ultimate fantasy of freedom. Clearly, mermaids are not just a Florida thing. But only here can you actually see them in the water in the flesh.

Back to Blood (2012)

Novel by Tom Wolfe

DOUBLING DOWN ON DIVERSITY

If best-selling, award-winning author and journalist Tom Wolfe was right, it doesn't matter whether you are Haitian, Latinx (although he didn't use the term), Anglo or Russian; it doesn't matter whether you live or work in Wynwood, Little Haiti, Hialeah, Little Havana, Mother Russia (also known as Sunny Isles and Hallandale), Fisher Island, Star Island, Liberty City, Little River, Buena Vista, Brownsville, Little Caracas (also known as Westonzuela) or any other neighborhood mentioned in his fourth and final novel. It doesn't matter if you're a cop, a politician, a journalist, a medical professional, an artist or a business tycoon. It doesn't matter if you are young and gorgeous or sport blue hair, a bent back and a walker. Fantastically rich or abysmally poor—that doesn't matter, either. In Tom Wolfe's Miami, everybody either looks down on or desperately wants to become somebody else—sometimes both at the same time.

According to Wolfe's publisher, *Back to Blood* is about "class, family, wealth, race, crime, sex, corruption and ambition in Miami, the city where America's future has arrived first." Judging by the book's acknowledgments, the author talked to everyone and went everywhere in the city to get his story—like the journalist he was at the onset of his career. He is inside the head, for instance, of the new managing editor of the *Miami Herald*, who thought he was publishing great investigative reporting, only to find that he had aggravated the wrong community. Which means that the second time

Author Tom Wolfe in his signature white suit at the White House. *Wikimedia Commons.*

he gets a chance to run with a good story, he thinks twice and then one hundred times more.

Early on, we meet protagonist Nestor Comancho, the strapping young Cuban cop who becomes a pariah to his community for heroically—in his own eyes, at least—following an order to rescue a refugee from a seventy-foot-tall flagpole before he fell and hurt himself. The problem for the Cubans watching was what is known as wet-foot/dry-foot, the U.S. policy governing Cuban refugees that states that those who set foot on American soil are allowed to stay and request parole; the following year, they can apply for residency. This is a source of endless frustration and fury for Haiti, incidentally, whose refugees tend to be summarily deported. It is also a reason that today, a full 60 percent of Miami-Dade County claims to be of Cuban origin.

It is this enmity, competition and refusal—maybe inability—to melt into one Miami, despite or because of the depictions of overpowering heat and humidity, that presaged the subsequent siloing of American politics. There was a time, short though it was, when many Americans could pretend that we almost actually *were* a melting pot. If indeed Wolfe's Miami showed where America's future lay, he knew that we were in for a lot more conflict. At the time Wolfe wrote the book, he notes Miami was the only city in the world that had a recent immigration rate of 50 percent.

Yet despite the background chaos, the book's most violent scene is a fistfight between two white businessmen that is staged for a reality show. I won't spoil the ending, but let's just say that the main character, for all his cultural cluelessness, could have ended up much, much worse.

Maybe that's a good omen for Miami—and for us—after all.

FUN FACT ABOUT *BACK TO BLOOD*

The publisher Little, Brown and Company reportedly paid Wolfe nearly $7 million for the book. Sadly, it was a financial failure.

Bad Boys (1995), *Bad Boys II* (2003), *Bad Boys for Life* (2020), *Bad Boys: Ride or Die* (2024)

Directed by Michael Bay, Adil El Arbi and Bilall Fallah; Starring Will Smith, Martin Lawrence, Joe Pantoliano, Theresa Randle, Dennis Greene, et al.

GOOD BUDDIES

It's the ultimate buddy movie. In the opening moments of the first *Bad Boys* flick, an odd couple of Miami police department detectives—Marcus Burnett, a goofy family man with big ears, and Mike Lowrey, a smooth-talking ladies' man driving a $100,000 (in 1995) Porsche—are in the process of being assaulted by a couple of tough characters. Within minutes, the pair, who were already bickering about Burnett's eating in the fancy car before the criminals showed up, yell so loudly *at each other* that the would-be carjackers are distracted and are thus easily overcome.

The movie is funny and action-packed, often with over-the-top violence. Otherwise, it's got drugs, guns, car chases, explosives and most of the other usual suspects you'll find in a Miami-based crime flick—as do all the others in the series, to a greater or lesser degree. But the humor and the relationship between the two cops, which was, at least at first, highly improvised, make all the difference—as do the hundreds of millions of dollars the franchise has made for its producers. And while the box office take has flagged with each sequel, at the time of this writing, *Ride or Die* has just recently opened. Will the magic prevail three decades later? And if it does, what does that say about Miami? What would a movie that's been described as a cross between

Martin Lawrence and Will Smith come to the rescue in *Bad Boys*. *RGR Collection/Alamy Stock Photo.*

one of the old-time Bob Hope/Bing Crosby road movies and *Lethal Weapon* add to our understanding of a place that *Miami Vice* did not?

Maybe it's the fact that in *Bad Boys*, both cops are Black, whereas in *Vice*, it was clearly Sonny Crockett who was the star, while Ricardo Tubbs tended to be portrayed as a sidelined sidekick. Or maybe it's just that sometimes it's all so bad that you just have to laugh.

Of course, you could make that same case about Los Angeles, the setting of the movies' TV spin-off, *L.A.'s Finest* (2019–20). It features cop Syd Burnett, played by Gabrielle Union, who was Marcus Burnett's sister in *Bad Boys II*.

But that's another city and another story altogether. All in all, there's nothing quite like *Bad Boys*. What you gonna do?

FUN FACTS ABOUT THE *BAD BOYS* FRANCHISE

The role of Mike Lowrey was first offered to Arsenio Hall, who turned it down, a decision he came to bitterly regret. Denzel Washington and Eddie

Murphy were also in the running to play the cops. Also, the first two films put Martin Lawrence's name first on advertising, while the last two gave top billing to Will Smith, who, by then, had become the far bigger star. And in *Ride or Die*, watch for the callback to Will Smith's 2022 Academy Awards slap-heard-round-the-world of Chris Rock. Suffice it to say, it's funny.

Because of Winn-Dixie (2005)

Film Directed by Wayne Wang; Starring Jeff Daniels,
AnnaSophia Robb, Cicely Tyson, Dave Matthews,
Eva Marie Saint and Elle Fanning

HAIR OF THE DOG

The dog actually *grins*. With that classic Berger Picard, or Picardy Shepherd, expression, a platonic love affair and a much-loved Florida movie take flight. Adapted from Kate DiCamillo's award-winning children's book of the same name, Wayne Wang's movie is the story of a lonely, motherless child named India "Opal" Buloni, who is plunked down in yet another small town due to her preacher father's job—this time, in fictional Naomi, Florida. There are few for her to befriend, either in her father's tiny convenience store/ house of worship or in her elementary school. That is until she meets the previously mentioned dog, whom she encounters busy wreaking havoc at, you guessed it, the local Winn-Dixie supermarket. That's what she names the stray, immediately claiming him as her own. It's only a matter of time before the town claims the child as their own, as well.

For those not in the know, the Winn-Dixie grocery chain goes back a century, first under a different name, and there have been Winn-Dixies serving customers in the South since 1955. Headquartered in Jacksonville, the business, founded by the Davis family, until recently boasted nearly 550 stores in Alabama, Georgia, Louisiana and Mississippi, in addition to Florida. (Recently, many of the stores were sold to the German supermarket chain Aldi.) In other words, it's nearly as Southern as fried chicken and mint juleps and as Floridian as orange juice.

Needless to say, the love affair between Opal and Winn-Dixie is star-crossed almost from the start. Trouble arrives in the form of the family's landlord, who won't allow dogs on the property. What ensues after that first provocation is the kind of movie in which an adorable dog wreaks havoc not once but three times, the second time among a monkey, a goose, rabbits, a pig and a parrot in a pet shop and the third time in church. It's not a spoiler to tell you that all ends happily ever after. After all, big-eyed Opal, played by newcomer AnnaSophia Robb, has us and her dad in the palm of her hands with the words, "He's the only friend I have."

Berger Picards like this little guy were in high demand after the success of *Because of Winn-Dixie*. *Image by DejaVu Designs on Freepik.*

Fabulous marketing for a supermarket chain, wouldn't you say?

FUN FACTS ABOUT *BECAUSE OF WINN-DIXIE*

A musical adaptation was produced in Arkansas. Also, the Berger Picard Club of America was formed shortly after the movie came out.

The Birdcage (1996)

Film Directed by Mike Nichols; Starring Robin Williams, Gene Hackman, Nathan Lane and Dianne Wiest

WILD CREATURES OF SOUTH BEACH

Many viewers agree: the spectacular opening tracking shot from the middle of the Atlantic Ocean to Miami Beach was worth the price of admission to this movie. And when audiences saw Robin Williams playing a straight man—you should excuse the expression—opposite his character's over-the-top flamboyant partner in life and in business Nathan Lane, they went wild for them both. *The Birdcage*, a remake of a remake (first a 1973 French play and then a 1978 French-Italian movie) is a comedy of manners that celebrates and pokes fun at everything from heterosexual families to drag shows and prejudice, Western masculine stereotypes and conservative ideology. It also showcases Miami Beach in all its glory.

Nichols had reportedly planned to shoot the film in New Orleans. Then he took one look at the South Beach drag scene and quickly changed his mind. Like many Florida movies, the interior scenes were shot in Los Angeles. No matter. We are still treated to that gorgeous skyline shot, plus the bikini and rollerblader–filled sidewalks of Ocean Drive, as well as the Carlyle Hotel and the famed Art Deco District.

Equally important are the people the movie puts front and center. Although the Wilton Manors neighborhood in Greater Fort Lauderdale is considered the gayest city in Florida and the second gayest in the nation, South Beach takes a lot of pride in its Pride. Today, it boasts an LGBT Visitors Center, two beaches that are well-known to cater to the gay community and plenty of drag shows and gay clubs.

It all fits in well with the plot. When a twenty-year-old man announces to his gay parents, one of whom owns a drag club and the other who is its featured star, that he plans to marry a woman, they are shocked enough. But when the young woman's U.S. senator father wants to use a meeting with the couple to distract from a political scandal that threatens his family values credentials, the gay couple goes into crisis mode. How does an effeminate man behave like a heterosexual man? How do you redecorate an apartment to look straight? While the script follows many of the scenes from the European original, director Mike Nichols dialed up the intensity of the gags, and his cowriter Elaine May added the subplot of the senator's political woes to interrogate American values at a time when gay marriage was illegal and representations of gay people in the media were still not quite mainstream.

In 1996, there had already been several movies featuring gay characters, but none had the broad appeal and subsequent box office success—grossing its investors six times their investment—of *The Birdcage*. It might have been the remarkable leads, along with a scene-stealing turn by Hank Azaria as the couple's Guatemalan housekeeper. Or the movie's theme of family love above all else. Still, it wouldn't be the same film without the Miami Beach's street cafés, wardrobe and, perhaps above all, climate. *The Birdcage* exudes sunshine toward the end of a very dark period for the gay community. While between 1982 and 1987, the Northeast had the largest share, 38 percent, of AIDS cases, soon after that, the South had the most, with 38 percent by the period in which the film came out.

Laughter was crucial, and *The Birdcage* delivered.

FUN FACTS ABOUT *THE BIRDCAGE*

Due to his usual on-screen antics, Robin Williams was first asked to play the Nathan Lane role, but he had just performed in drag in *Mrs. Doubtfire*. Also, Steve Martin was asked to play the character, but he didn't think he could do justice to it.

Bloodline (2015–17)

TV Series Created by Todd A. Kessler, Glenn Kessler and
Daniel Zelman; Starring Ben Mendelsohn,
Kyle Chandler, Linda Cardellini and Sissy Spacek

FAMILY SECRETS

From the award-winning creators of the out-for-blood lawyer Patty Hewes
in *Damages* came another double-entendre-titled thriller series, *Bloodline*,
about bad blood among blood relatives. The primary setting is a charming,
family-owned inn in the Upper Keys, and the plot centers on the return of
the family's black sheep elder son and the consciences of his detective and
marina owner younger brothers, as well as that of his attorney sister.

While the foremost pleasure to be had from *Bloodline* may be the (at least
initially) compelling storyline and always extraordinary cast (stars like Sam
Shepard, John Leguizamo, Andrea Riseborough and Chloë Sevigny, among
others, take their bows), the lovely old seaside hotel serves as a metaphor for
the stability of a certain kind of Florida family: longstanding natives who
truly belong to the land. Far from short-term tourism and the stereotypical
retirement condos, drug dealing or boiler room mentality of some non-
natives, these characters have a stake in these parts, even if not all of them
always feel like they belong in the family. The tragedy of the property's
being used for something it shouldn't is not only that it compromises nice
people and leads to all kinds of mayhem, but that it also signals the loss of
a wholesome way of life. Although this was by no means always the case,
violent crime was not generally considered a feature as opposed to a bug of
Old Florida—at least not among what we might think of as good middle-

class families. *Bloodline*'s Sally and Robert Rayburn are no saints, not by a long shot. The case could even be made that their eldest son's lawbreaking was directly related to Robert's abuse. Nevertheless, they were able to create a foundation and a legacy that was out of reach for future generations of Rayburns, even their three younger children, who, at first and second glance, had actually made good.

Bloodline, then, can be seen as an elegy for a lifestyle that not many people got to enjoy in the first place, but that was certainly part of the Florida landscape for a good long time.

FUN FACT ABOUT *BLOODLINE*

The series didn't get canceled for the usual reason (that is, poor ratings). In fact, the reviews were generally quite positive. It just got too expensive to shoot on location in the Florida Keys. And without the location, the show would never be the same.

Body Heat (1981)

Film Directed by Lawrence Kasdan; Starring William Hurt, Kathleen Turner, Richard Crenna and Ted Danson

FEVERISH

The first part of this movie—when daring passions flare and dastardly plans are hatched—is mainly bathed in red, from the opening fire to William Hurt's red car and red shirts, Kathleen Turner's red skirt, the red wallpaper in the bar and the red cherry pie, not to mention plenty of red mood lighting. Not that we need to be reminded of the kind of heat that turns a hapless lover into an even more hapless murderer, particularly in South Florida, when it's hard to think straight during a steamy summer at the best of times. In the original story, *Double Indemnity*, the protagonist is a feckless insurance salesman; here, he's a lawyer not wholly unfamiliar with malpractice who falls head over heels for the same twenty-seven-year-old woman who captivated all of America at the time of this, her debut film. Kathleen Turner, soon to be called one of the "100 Sexiest Stars in Film History," could probably make nearly anyone capable of murder.

Interestingly, the movie, based on the James M. Cain novel and the Fred MacMurray/Barbara Stanwyck movie of the same name—both of which were set in Los Angeles—wasn't supposed to take place in Florida. Miami native Kasdan made the switch after an actors' strike delayed filming in Los Angeles. Lake Worth, a small city situated south of West Palm Beach, takes pride of place as the fictional Miranda Beach, although there were ultimately a number of South Florida locations that appeared on screen. Speaking of making the cut, the movie was even steamier when it was first screened for a small audience. However, it likely would not have escaped an

X rating—the kiss of death for feature films seeking wide distribution—had it not been edited.

So, it was pretty much the luck of the draw that *Body Heat* was a Florida movie—and yet maybe not. This neo-noir is about a lot of things, but it primarily focuses on greed and exploitation, two themes that appear again and again in Florida's history, as well as in its fiction. It could just as easily have been called "Hunger," except that the characters didn't eat a lot, apart from the aforementioned cherry pie. On the other hand, who knows? Without those sweat-stained shirts and the perspiration pouring down those beautiful bodies, maybe audiences wouldn't have bought the attraction?

Nah, it was still Kathleen Turner and William Hurt at their best. They could have been wearing snow suits and caused the sparks to fly.

FUN FACTS ABOUT *BODY HEAT*

Although the movie takes place in the scorching heat of a South Florida summer, it was actually filmed in November, and it was freezing. It was not what you'd call an easy shoot. Also, future disgraced U.S. representative Mark Foley was hired on as an extra.

The Body in Question (2019)

Novel by Jill Ciment

SIX ANGRY MEN AND WOMEN

University of Florida professor and award-winning writer Jill Ciment draws on her own May-December marriage in this tale of jurors in trouble in Central Florida. The story follows a sequestered jury's experience during the trial of a possibly autistic young woman accused of setting fire to her family home and killing her infant brother inside—as well as the trial's aftermath. Apart from the sexual relationship the married main character Hannah (known in the first half of the book by her jury name, C-2) forges with another juror, the story gives a number of interesting insights into the Florida court system and beyond. For instance: Aren't juries supposed to contain twelve people?

Only six states allow six-person juries as opposed to the usual twelve: Arizona, Connecticut, Florida, Indiana, Massachusetts and Utah. And these trials require unanimous verdicts. In the case of Florida, which has allowed a six-person jury since 1970, twelve people are seated on a jury only for a criminal case eligible for the death penalty. The state's highly controversial six-person jury quota recently came to national attention when George Zimmerman was tried for the murder of Trayvon Martin in 2013.

Due to the jury shenanigans described in this novel, one might be predisposed to the need for more jurors. (At one point, Hannah/C-2 suggests that she should sleep with her fellow juror just so they can concentrate once more on the trial. Clearly, all hands are needed on deck.) These six (plus an alternate, who serves on the jury when another lies to the judge about sleeping through part of the trial) have more on their minds than guilt or innocence—or maybe it's just not the guilt or innocence of the accused that is consuming their attention. In any case, following a Florida trial, jurors' names and addresses are compiled by the clerk of court, as are their answers from the jury selection process, known as *voir dire*, and these are made generally available to the public. Needless to say, this detail causes great headaches for the accused among the jury in *The Body in Question*.

Incidentally, Ciment set her story in the vicinity of The Villages, an eighty-thousand-person retirement community in Central Florida's Marion and Sumter Counties. About thirty-two square miles in size, it is itself the subject of books, articles and even a documentary extolling the benefits and bemoaning the hazards of the area's meticulously planned, overwhelmingly conservative lifestyle. Outside the pristine landscaping of The Villages are the usual seedy family diners, Olive Gardens and Econo Lodges that the jury must make use of during its sequestration.

If there is a connection among older/younger relationships (Hannah is thirty-four years younger than her husband and a decade older than her juror of choice), retirement communities, strip mall capitalism, adultery and the Florida justice system, perhaps it's this: wherever we are and whoever we are, we can only try to do the best we can with what we have. And we can only ask the same from everyone else.

The Bone Cay (2021)

Novel by Eliza Nellums

IS THERE A HISTORIAN IN THE HOUSE?

In 2017, a record 6.5 million Floridians evacuated the state in advance of Hurricane Irma, a category 5 (above 156 miles-per-hour winds) storm. The curator and staff of the historic Hemingway Home and Museum in Key West were not among them. Neither were the famous six-toed cats that prowl the grounds.

The story helped inspire Nellums's slow-burn thriller, which takes place at the fictional Whimbrel Estate in Key West, home of the (also fictional) acclaimed poet Isobel Reyes. Reyes, as every schoolchild in the area knew, killed herself there in 1918 at age twenty-three. In four days of preparation for the storm and in horror at its intensity, curator Magda Trudell, a historian, botanist and Reyes obsessive, discovers not only the truth about Reyes's death but also the hidden strength she couldn't have known she herself possessed.

There's a truism that there are four main conflicts in literature: man (or in this case woman) against man, man against nature, man against supernatural and man against self. *The Bone Cay*, which takes its name from the Spanish settlers' term for the area, *Cayo Hueso*, or Bone Island—for the Native Calusa bones found there—pits Magda against all four. Her skills, quick thinking and sheer strength of character, especially when an acquaintance shows up with a pregnant fifteen-year-old and throws her carefully laid plans to the raging winds, are formidable.

And really, who better to handle it all than an academic? As a historian, she knows what valuables in the house need to be saved, including a rotting trunk with a mysterious passenger unearthed by the storm. As a botanist, she can identify every inch of the property, save cuttings from a historic lime tree and use native plants for healing. And as a quick thinker, she manages to save her own life and those of the innocent. Including, incidentally, the book's answer to those Hemingway cats: four lemurs. Through it all, Magda is as resilient as the mangroves that help prevent her from drowning. Sort of like we all hope Florida will be as the climate crisis escalates.

How many people *The Bone Cay* convinces to evacuate during the next big hurricane, no one can say. But the vivid hell-on-Earth scenario reminds readers that, at least in Florida, nature is a formidable opponent.

FUN FACT ABOUT *THE BONE CAY*

There is a character named Isabel Reyes (with an "a") in the movie *Sicario: Day of the Soldado*, played by Isabela Moner. There's no relation, as far as can be made out.

Boynton Beach Club (2006)

Film Directed by Susan Seidelman; Starring Dyan Cannon, Joseph Bologna, Len Cariou and Michael Nouri

SIXTY CANDLES

The real Valencia Isles is a gated, fifty-five-plus community of more than one thousand homes spread over 450 acres in West Boynton, 16 miles southwest of Palm Beach. If Susan Seidelman's movie is to be believed, the community, built between 2002 and 2008, was, at least at one time, a hotbed of hot sex, although not necessarily for its own sake. If there was any question about what's on the mind of many of these characters, the movie's opening theme is Sinatra's "Love and Marriage."

The club in question, it should be noted, is not a beach club; rather, it is a bereavement group located in one of many luxurious senior communities west of Boynton Beach. Seidelman got the idea from true stories she heard from her mother, Florence, who wrote a treatment for the screenplay. Florence also raised money, cast the extras and did the marketing—more than earning her a producer credit.

What distinguishes this movie from any other romantic comedy that buys into the boy-meets-girl archetype is, of course, the age of the boys and girls. Viagra, widowhood, divorce and aging bodies were not the usual concerns of romantic comedies in 2006, and they aren't much more prominent now. Then there are the things these seniors *do* have in common with their grandchildren: loneliness, depression, fear, condoms, dildos, porn and, yes, even smoking pot. It seems that unlike the vastly more popular movie *Cocoon*, *Beach Club* reminds us that those people you see walking the mall, strutting their stuff at water aerobics and bargain-hunting at the flea market really aren't that different from you or me. They even—at least if you're Kellerman or Cannon—may look better, especially when doing the twist at a '50s-themed dance. Speaking of which: at one point, Kellerman, age sixty-nine at the time, briefly bares her chest, a nice flashback to her famous shower scene as Hot Lips Houlihan in the movie *M*A*S*H*. Whether it's a mark of her character's desperation or free spirit, it works for her as it works for us.

Perhaps the most authentic scene in the movie, however, comes toward the end, when Brenda Vaccaro's Marilyn slaps the dreadful, orange-tanned woman (Renée Taylor) who fatally backed her car into Marilyn's husband at the start. There's life after sixty in Florida, for sure. But it isn't all bosom buddies and roses.

FUN FACTS ABOUT *BOYNTON BEACH CLUB*

Florence Seidelman's friend David Cramer from another West Boynton community, Palm Isles, joined a synagogue bereavement group when his wife, Florence's best friend, Marilyn, died. In the movie, Len Cariou and Sally Kellerman play David and the partner he met there. And the heart of the film is a widow named Marilyn, one of the people to whom the movie is dedicated. Also, Florence Seidelman gave her friend Lois a small speaking part in the movie during a bereavement group scene.

Burn Notice (2007-13)

Created by Max Nix; Starring Jeffrey Donovan, Gabrielle Anwar, Bruce Campbell, Sharon Gless and Coby Bell

BYE SPY

A man stands on a street corner, incongruously dressed in a white shirt and gray suit in the middle of the colorful, bustling city of Warri in southern Nigeria. Soon, he is unceremoniously placed in the back of a black Mercedes by two strong young men, who are immune to his quips about the carmaker's latest model. When he meets a man identified onscreen as "Boris Wannabe Warlord," we know that we have nothing to fear. We understand that the suit, who we quickly learn is a spy suddenly hung out to dry by his handlers in the middle of a dangerous transaction, is, despite a few ugly bruises, going be just fine. What's the worst that can happen? Ah, yes. He is flown to Miami.

Burn Notice is the saga of Michael Westen, a wisecracking former special forces operator and now former spy who has no idea why the ghosts at his job are now ghosting *him*. We find out why in season two, and surprisingly, it's got nothing to do with his wry sense of humor, which, in fact, audiences seemed to like. By 2010, viewers ranked the show no. 2 for scripted shows on cable, with an audience of as much as 6.7 million per episode. It also won a few awards, including a Best Supporting Actress Emmy for veteran Sharon Gless.

Why do they send Westen to Miami? As he explains in his frequent voiceovers, spies are "burned" when they are no longer considered useful to the organization. They are left adrift with no job history, money or contacts.

And home is the place that's got to take you in when no one else will. The series, which concerns the ex-spy's efforts to unravel the mystery of his new nonexistence while working as a private investigator to stay afloat, is also a meditation on the meaning of home. We know how some people feel about their hometowns, especially those trying to steer clear of memories of their abusive childhoods. (Fortunately, Dad is gone, and Mom ends up being more of a help than a hindrance.) *Burn Notice* is thus the story of a spy who very reluctantly came out of the cold, only to face the warmth and sunshine of a place so many consider paradise, but which has long spelled danger for him. So, just as he did as a kid, he is constantly scouting out threats, if not from criminals, then from the feds who are pledged to keep him in check.

What we learn from *Burn Notice*, ultimately, is that there's no place like home. And that goes double for Miami.

FUN FACTS ABOUT *BURN NOTICE*

Star Jeffrey Donovan has a scar under his left eye. Series writers wrote it into the script, explaining it was a memento from Westen's abusive father. Also, the show's creator, Nix, has a speaking part in every title sequence. He's the one who says, "We got a burn notice on you. You're blacklisted."

Camino Winds (2017)

Novel by John Grisham

THE PATH TO MURDER

In Spanish, *camino* means "path," and it looks like no. 1 *New York Times* bestselling author John Grisham has found yet another literary path paved with gold, this time in Florida. With his Camino books, the Destin homeowner and author and of *The Firm* and *A Time to Kill* and dozens more takes his legal thriller audience outside the courtroom and into the bookstore, Bay Books, to be exact, owned by one Bruce Cable. The popular retailer, located in the fictional beach town of Santa Rosa (there's a real one in the Panhandle) on Northeast Florida's equally fictional Camino Island, is a community hub. And with all the crime-fighting that goes on in and around the store, it's a wonder any books get sold at all.

We first meet Cable in the novel *Camino Island*. A sort of pied piper of local writers, he skillfully skirts the law while stashing a small fortune he's earned from dealing in rare books of questionable provenance. Mercer Mann is a young writer with ties to the island who is paid to deliver him to the authorities—and fails. In the latest installment in the series, *Camino Ghosts*, Cable involves Mann in a story complete with greedy developers and—you guessed it—an apparent poltergeist. Over the course of the books, Mercer becomes a bestselling novelist in her own right and a dear friend to Cable.

It's the second book, however, *Camino Winds*, that truly feels like an only-in-Florida mystery. Opening with a devastatingly true-to-life description of the wait, the worry and the woe that is a category 4 hurricane, the book provides enough large-scale Medicare fraud, drug company shenanigans, nursing home abuses, alcohol and raw oysters to satisfy any Floridaholic. Not to mention a murder during the storm that the hapless local police initially classify as yet another homeowner-versus-hurricane mishap.

Like Grisham's other books, the *Camino* series is good fun, if not great literature. Unlike them, however, it delivers a solid picture of the laid-back yet privileged life of affluent locals in a Florida resort town. Even tracking down murderers is done with a certain joie de vivre. The books are by and large good-humored romps that go down as easily as one of the many, many beers enjoyed by the characters.

FUN FACTS ABOUT *CAMINO WINDS*

In the novel, Grisham twice refers in passing to Scott Turow, a literary competitor. Also, the town of Santa Rosa on Camino Island bears a striking resemblance to Fernandina Beach on Amelia Island, about an hour from Jacksonville, which figures prominently in the plot. Both are on the east coast of the state and just miles from the Georgia border.

Cocoon (1985)

Film Directed by Ron Howard; Starring Don Ameche,
Wilford Brimley, Hume Cronyn, Brian Dennehy,
Jack Gilford, Steve Guttenberg, Maureen Stapleton,
Jessica Tandy, Gwen Verdon and Tahnee Welch

NO MORE EARLY BIRD SPECIALS

Make no mistake, *Cocoon* was not your father's everyday, run-of-the-mill
ensemble flick about seniors magically revitalized by swimming in a pool
filled with alien cocoons. With its almost all-star cast of Hollywood icons
and A-listers, its gorgeous St. Petersburg location and heartwarming Ron
Howard direction, the movie reaped mostly positive reviews, two Academy
Awards (including for best supporting actor, Don Ameche, who started in
vaudeville and was seventy-seven years old at the film's premiere) and a less
well-received 1988 sequel, *Cocoon: The Return.*

Just what was it about *Cocoon* that captured the imaginations of moviegoers
in the 1980s and causes it to remain a canny examination of Florida life even
today? To be sure, the stellar cast and beloved former child star director don't
hurt. But *Cocoon* also combines the Sunshine State's persistent stereotype
as a waiting room for heaven or elsewhere with the centuries-old myth of
Florida as the site of the Fountain of Youth. It allows us to imagine an
alternative present in which graying seniors trudging to early bird specials
and shuffleboard courts suddenly kick up their heels and breakdance. Not
to mention their sex drives. In the mid-1980s, at the height of the careers
of health and fitness gurus like Jane Fonda and Richard Simmons and
the threshold of a bold new era of cosmetic surgery—Botox as a wrinkle

treatment was discovered two years after the film's release—the excitement around this movie was in large part related to the exponential rise of real-life techniques for forestalling the symptoms of aging. And the fantasy surrounding that possibility certainly still holds meaning for people today—maybe even more so.

In the film, the Florida retirees who trespass in their alien neighbors' pool not only benefit from the water's rejuvenating power (think cavorting seniors) but also destroy it. Their only hope to remain youthful and immortal is to follow the aliens back to their home planet. What does that tell us about our culture's search for the modern-day Fountain of Youth on Earth? Suffice it to say, it doesn't bode well.

Tourists and newcomers to the state may, depending upon where they land, be shocked to discover the existence of elementary schools and universities in this popular retirement destination. But take my word for it: just like anywhere else, Florida has its share of young and old, working and retired, beautiful and less so. That's what's called a community. Cities like Boca "Botox" Raton may hold out the promise of eternal youth, but we will always have—and hopefully always celebrate—the elders among us. And inside us. Because one day, we, too, will grow older and die. *Cocoon*'s take on this news can be summed up in four little words: get used to it.

But there's another message in the film about Florida and beyond that continues to delight and comfort audiences. As his elders take off into space, young Ben, played by Steve Guttenberg, sails back to a land of blue skies, rolling waves and impressive St. Pete locations, including the historic Snell Arcade building, which has stood the test of time since 1926. Then in the film's final scene, David, the grandson of Wilford Brimley's character, stands at the funeral of the seniors who are presumed to be dead. Looking up at the sky, the child smiles in the knowledge that Grandpa and his pals are not only alive but will also never die. Do we then mourn for David and Ben, who are destined for another path? Not at all. Because for their generation, there is still plenty of healthy aging ahead. Florida restaurants have since rebranded early bird specials. Now, they're called sunset dinners. And if you look at the diners enjoying them today—thanks to the miracle of medicine, nutrition and exercise—they are break-dancing nearly as well as Don Ameche.

FUN FACTS ABOUT *COCOON*

Did you see that gorgeous young alien? She was played by Raquel Welch's daughter Tahnee. Also, a then-twenty-seven-year-old Steve Guttenberg received a DUI conviction during the filming of the movie, but he was quickly let off by a starstruck constabulary. What's more, grizzled character actor and longtime Quaker Oats shill Wilford Brimley, who was forty-nine when the film was shot, had to be made up to look older. Brimley died in 2020 at the ripe old age of eighty-five. Seems like the alien planet couldn't keep those oldsters hopping after all. Not to worry. They achieved immortality due in part to their appearances in this great film—not to mention that they got to spend some quality time in Florida.

Cold Florida (2016)

Novel by Phillip DePoy

THE LOST TRIBES

In the terse, clever narration of a hard-boiled gumshoe with the overtones of a college graduate and Borscht Belt *kibitzer,* Foggy Moscowitz, a car thief turned Child Protective Services officer, relates the incidents of a few eventful days in his life during the winter of 1974. But this is not your father's Florida mystery-thriller. Foggy is a Brooklyn Jewish man in his forties. Like the Seminoles before him, who populated his newly adopted town of Fry's Bay, Foggy has come to Florida against his will. In the case of the Seminole Natives, being the only tribe who did not capitulate to the U.S. government in the nineteenth century, it was a matter of being forced into a smaller and smaller piece of land until the only real estate they could hold onto was the forbidding Everglades. In the case of Foggy, suffice it to say, he did something back North that turned out to be very, very wrong, and he was on the lam. He was not the first Floridian to arrive under those terms, and he was certainly not the last.

Nothing like hiding in plain sight. By 1974, Florida wasn't exactly the last frontier, and a government job wasn't a cave. Foggy is just getting off work past midnight when he receives an urgent assignment to track down a junkie and her newborn, who have escaped from the maternity ward. If the drug-addicted baby doesn't get medicine soon, she'll die. With that nail-biting setup, Foggy goes on to talk, strong-arm and/or hotwire his way into and out of nearly every crisis that arises. And there are plenty, many of which involve that proud Florida tribe.

The exact location of the fictional Fry's Bay is not divulged, but it is clearly on the edges of what is now Big Cypress National Preserve, the development of which figures prominently in the plot. We learn that most everyone in town has a Seminole relative, and we know that virtually all of the two thousand or so Seminoles in Florida live in one of six reservations: Hollywood and Ft. Pierce on the east coast, Big Cypress and Brighton in Central Florida and Immokalee and Tampa on the west coast. The delightful evocations of place and personality make this book come alive, even when most of the bad guys are dead.

Fortunately, Foggy prevails. He's got to. There are, at the time of this writing, three more books in DePoy's Foggy Moscowitz series.

FUN FACT ABOUT PHILLIP DEPOY

Although Phillip DePoy has published twenty-one novels, he's had more than twice as many of his plays produced. His play *Easy* won an Edgar Award, the premier prize for mysteries.

Cool Hand Luke (1965)

Novel by Donn Pearce

Cool Hand Luke (1967)

Film Directed by Stuart Rosenberg; Starring Paul Newman, George Kennedy, J.D. Cannon and Robert Drivas

A FAILURE TO COMMUNICATE

A decade before the novel *One Flew Over the Cuckoo's Nest* was the basis of a zeitgeist-capturing film about an outsider fighting "the Man," there was *Cool Hand Luke*. The movie, starring Hollywood icon Paul Newman as the egg-eating World War II hero incarcerated in 1950s Florida for decapitating parking meters, racked up a slew of Oscar nominations, a best supporting actor win for George Kennedy and an almost unheard-of 100 percent on Rotten Tomatoes. Not to mention that the Library of Congress considered it "culturally, historically, or aesthetically significant" enough for preservation in the National Film Registry.

The movie takes place in the early 1950s, but chain gangs were long a significant feature of incarceration in the American South. Thirty years after they were phased out in the United States, Florida, which began the practice in 1919, became the third state to reinstitute the punishment, which it renamed "restricted labor gangs." Florida's practice of putting prisoners to work in turpentine camps or building railroads for little or no pay through the convict lease program dates to the period following the Civil War, and even today, prisoners in Florida and other states are part of the workforce behind many of the major brands found in supermarkets.

Cool Hand Luke—the character receives the moniker after winning a hand of poker on a bluff—is memorable for many reasons. Besides exposing the corrupt and harrowing side of prison life, it features Paul Newman's rendition of the 1957 folk song "Plastic Jesus," written by Ed Rush and George Cromarty, which apparently wasn't recorded until 1962, after the movie is set. And then there's that astonishing egg scene, in which our hero eats fifty hardboiled eggs in an hour. (It's believed that the actor actually consumed "just" eight.)

Although Luke wins the respect and friendship of even the most hardened criminals at the prison, he never stops plotting ill-conceived escape plans, particularly after the death of his mother. The film's sobering conclusion reminds us that despite the movie hijinks, incarceration in Florida is certainly no laughing matter.

FUN FACTS ABOUT *COOL HAND LUKE*

According to novelist Pearce, about one-third of the story is based on his own experiences serving two years in Florida Department of Corrections chain gangs after a 1949 burglary conviction for safecracking. He had previously been imprisoned in France for passing counterfeit money but escaped from a work detail. Also, the famous phrase uttered by prison warden Strother Martin ("What we've got here is a failure to communicate.") is ranked no. 11 on the list of the one hundred most memorable movie quotations compiled by the American Film Institute.

Cross Creek (1983)

Film Directed by Martin Ritt; Starring Mary Steenburgen, Rip Torn, Peter Coyote, Dana Hill and Keith Michel

LITTLE HOUSE IN THE ORANGE GROVE

Perhaps the movie version of *Yearling* author Marjorie Kinnan Rawlings's memoir about life around the Alachua County community known as Cross Creek and located about twenty miles southeast of Gainesville shouldn't be included in this compendium of Florida fiction. After all, Rawlings was a real person who really did leave her home and job in the Northeast to move to a seventy-two-acre orange grove in the late 1920s, where she lived in a nineteenth-century, Cracker-style farmhouse out in the semi-wilderness and came to a deep knowledge of the land and the people she found there. She really did become close to a backwoods family who taught her the ways of the nearby "Big Scrub" area of what became Ocala National Forest well enough for her to write about them. She did marry a local named Norton Baskin, and she did love to cook. Her first Florida story was, in fact, "Jacob's Ladder." And her editor was the literary giant Maxwell Perkins, who guided the careers of such luminaries as Fitzgerald, Hemingway and Wolfe.

Otherwise, however, a good deal of the film, unlike, presumably, the memoir, is fiction. Perhaps most importantly, Rawlings did not leave her husband when he refused to join her in her rural adventure; they in fact divorced after several years of living in Florida, making her a good deal less independent than she appears. The local family's name was Long, not Turner, as the movie would have it. And although the film implies that

Charles and Marjorie Kinnan Rawlings. *1940/State Archives of Florida.*

Rawlings had not sold a story before the fateful dinner when Perkins fell in love with "Jacob's Ladder," she was in fact already published.

The film does celebrate one aspect of the memoir that is definitely true-to-life, and it does so in living color: Rawlings's love of the land is palpable. It's true that few who see the movie may choose to drop everything and commit to the hard slog of reclaiming deserted land and orange groves, particularly at a time when far fewer processes were mechanized. (On the opening page of her memoir, she notes a conversation she had about how crazy it was to be living there.) Still, it's hard not to imagine what Rawlings must have seen: a pristine, albeit harsh, environment in which local people, flora and fauna coexisted. In which people relied on their neighbors for dang near everything—and educated, sophisticated ways wouldn't get you far when your very existence was on the line.

Happily, it doesn't all have to be left to the imagination. To a large extent, the rural nature of Cross Creek has been preserved along with Rawlings's home. At the end of her book, the author asks who owns Cross Creek, and the short answer is the State of Florida. Marjorie Kinnan Rawlings State Park is located in and around the author's Florida homestead. The building, the core of which is an original dogtrot house—that is, one or two raised, one-story log cabins under a single roof, connected by a breezeway—is a national historic landmark that has been open to the public since 1970. It is a testament to a way of life that made the state what it is today.

FUN FACT ABOUT *CROSS CREEK*

Rawlings's actual husband, Norton Baskin, has a small speaking part in the film when Marjorie asks him how to get a cab after first arriving in Cross Creek.

CSI: Miami (2002-12)

TV Series Created by Anthony E. Zulker, Ann Donahue, Carol Mendelsohn; Starring David Caruso, Emily Procter and Adam Rodriguez

THE KING OF THE ONE-LINERS

Laugh all you like about the Horatio Caine sunglasses meme—the many, many instances when star David Caruso makes a pithy statement while donning his Silhouette-brand shades at the onset of an episode—it apparently worked. In the grand tradition of the granddaddy of the long-lived CSI empire, *CSI: Crime Scene Investigation* (followed by *CSI: Miami*, *CSI: New York*, *CSI: Las Vegas* and the movie *CSI: Immortality*), the second iteration mixed a decidedly no-nonsense police procedural with just the slightest hint of a wink at the genre. Add in some stunning cinematography, sound editing and stunts (all of which won it Primetime Emmys), and you have a relative class act. In fact, at one point, it was, according to the BBC, the world's most popular TV show, based on the fact that it appeared in the top ten rankings of more countries than any other.

But why? Was it Caruso's particular combination of cuteness, condescension, cognition and, for a few seasons, conscience? Was it the (mostly) California locations? (To be fair, some of the shooting was done on location.) The "Won't Get Fooled Again" theme song? Personally, I'm putting my money on the look: the way the star's signature red hair coordinated with those hot sunsets and contrasted with those cold blue interiors. Miami is, after all, a lot about getting the right look.

It's another day, another crime for David Caruso in *CSI: Miami*. *Collection Christophel/Alamy Stock Photo.*

Caruso's Caine, the focal point of the show, is a veteran police lieutenant who directs the fictional Miami-Dade Crime Lab. Handy with a gun, he also knows his way around bombs. His ethnically and gender diverse team is also skilled, if generally younger. They have their issues and their entanglements, some of them with Caine himself, who marries the sister of a coworker, only to lose her. Above all, however, *CSI: Miami* is about the work, the painstaking process of determining in the lab, in the morgue and at the scene of the crime, why people breathed their last in the Everglades, South Beach or any other spectacular location.

The show made an impact. It has such legs that it was mentioned more than a decade later in the 2023 movie *Hit Man*—as, incidentally, was *Miami Vice*. Think of it as the nerd's version of *Vice*, with a pricey, if less cool, brand of sunglasses.

FUN FACT ABOUT *CSI: MIAMI*

Can't get enough of the show? Its spin-offs include video games, comics and novels.

A Dark and Lonely Place (2011)

Novel by Edna Buchanan

THE MORE THINGS CHANGE...

Who better to write crime novels set in South Florida than a former crime reporter for the *Miami Herald*? Although to most of the world, Pulitzer Prize winner (for journalism) Edna Buchanan is best known for her fictional tales of mayhem, as a reporter, she covered literally thousands of homicides. One she did not report on, however—at least in part because it occurred fifteen years before her birth—figures prominently in *A Dark and Lonely Place*. And it is, literally, the stuff of legend.

On November 1, 1924, John Ashley and several of his cronies were mowed down by members of the Palm Beach County Sheriff's Department, including the sheriff himself, Bob Baker. The murder on the Sebastian Bridge may or may not have been caused by the (handcuffed!) malefactors' attempted flight, but it did succeed in ending the reign of terror of the bootlegging pirates, bank robbers and murderers that comprised the Ashley Gang. Shortly after, John's gun moll Laura Upthegrove, the Bonnie to his Clyde, killed herself.

Buchanan's clever novel toggles back and forth between a liberty-taking retelling of the legend and her own completely fictional, present-day Miami murder case, in which Ashley's descendant, Homicide Sergeant John Ashley, finds himself accused of the crime. Even though Buchanan's series featuring the Cuban American reporter Britt Montero is extremely popular, it's the history and mystery that makes this particular novel so wonderfully emblematic of Florida fiction. *Lonely Place* blends together the true, the legendary—that is, based on truth but not fully verifiable—and the purely made up. As a matter of fact, that's a lot like the state itself.

Perhaps ironically, Buchanan herself was portrayed in fictionalized TV movie versions of her autobiography by Elizabeth Montgomery—although she claims pretty much all they used from the book was her name. And speaking of fiction, we might also consider some of the con artists who sold swampland in the 1920s. Or some of the shenanigans of the local businessmen and politicians, including those who wined and dined the likes of Al Capone. We might also look beneath the Botox of some of the Miami fashion models, who are, incidentally, well represented in the novel. What we'll find is a whole lot of smoke alongside some of those three-way mirrors. So much so that since 1967, Florida has boasted a "Sunshine Law" to prevent private backroom dealings in government. Not that it's always followed.

Of course, like any crime novel set in Miami, this one also reminds readers that not only fraud but also homicide have long been as much a part of the Florida landscape as the ocean tides and palm trees. One thing is sure: truth is still stranger than fiction—especially in Florida.

FUN FACT ABOUT EDNA BUCHANAN

Buchanan is haunted by the old, unsolved cases that she came across in her eighteen years of reporting crime. Sometimes, she solves these crimes in her fiction. Also, Elizabeth Montgomery asked Buchanan for a photocopy of the "I Love Miami" necklace she wore so she could have an identical one made by a jeweler to wear when she portrayed her.

Dark Light (2006)

Novel by Randy Wayne White

WRECKED

Call them salvors, or wreckers or just plain treasure hunters. Just don't call them later than you call their competitors if you've got knowledge of an old ship that's been underwater for quite some time. Because in Florida, salvage is serious business.

When Spanish explorers sailed to the New World, they tended to plunder the silver and gold valuables from the Inca and Aztec empires to take back home. Many of them never managed to survive the return trip, whether due to pirates, coastal or weather conditions or simply bad luck. That's where the modern-day treasure hunters come in. The most famous of them in Florida was Mel Fisher (1922–1998), who is best known for discovering the *Nuestra Señora de Atocha*, which was wrecked in 1622 near the Keys. The haul: $450 million. You can even buy a piece of what was on board. As an icon in the field, Fisher is name dropped in *Dark Light*, a story about a more recent and less real wreck, as is famous salvor Kip Wagner.

In the novel, Randy Wayne White, a former fishing guide at Tarpon Bay Marina, puts the wrecker industry (only a pastime for some) under the microscope as he explains about the use and abuse of salvage laws—some of them perfectly sensible, some of them downright ugly. The bestselling author has published about sixty works of fiction and nonfiction, including more than two dozen novels featuring the Gulf Coast–based marine biologist and retired NSA agent "Doc" Marion D. Ford. This one involves a hurricane that unearths a 1944 wreck just forty feet below the surface: a thirty-eight-foot

Shipwrecks, like this one in Stuart from 1890, are a boon for wreckers like those in *Dark Light. State Archives of Florida.*

Matthews that may or may not have been involved in either espionage, a plot to rescue German POWs from the camp in Fort Myers or both. The Sanibel Lighthouse, built for the war, plays a part, as do Nazi artifacts, Thomas Edison, Henry Ford and Charles Lindbergh. In the course of the action, White explains, among other things, the rumored wrecked U-boat off the coast of Sanibel, World War II coast watch boats and beach patrols, the science of cleaning artifacts, Florida's "Stand Your Ground" law, the toll a lightning strike takes on the body and how sketchy marinas can illegally claim millions of dollars of customers' property as their own, post-hurricane salvage. There's also a serial killer, one dead beauty and one who is very much alive, more storms than anyone needs and a host of interesting Gulf Coast characters.

Throughout, Wayne makes some very interesting points about age, whether of valuables or people. Does age make a difference? Is it all a matter of how we look at a thing or in what light, figuratively as well as literally? In examining the question, we are also struck by the nature of truth. Big questions for a thriller. But then this is a thriller chock-full of information, and it's not all about Florida.

FUN FACT ABOUT *DARK LIGHT*

Randy Wayne White has a restaurant chain named after his hero. Doc Ford's Rum Bar and Grille has four locations: two in St. Petersburg, one on Sanibel Island and one on Fort Myers Beach.

The Deep Blue Good-by (1964)

Novel by John D. MacDonald

FORT LAUDERDALE FOREVER

If you read only one grisly, deeply cynical and disturbing crime novel about Florida, make it this one. Before there was Barry, Buchanan or Hiassen, there was MacDonald, enshrined in the annals of the state's crime fiction six decades ago with the first of a twenty-one-book series about the intrepid army vet and "salvage consultant" Travis McGee. But don't take my word for it. He's Dean Koontz's favorite novelist ever, and Stephen King called him "the great entertainer of our age."

Good-by comes with the requisite backstabbing World War II army buddy, serial rapist, buried treasure in the Keys and femme fatale. MacDonald's publisher, which requested a series character, held onto the first installment until the author handed over two more. The three books came out one a month over the course of three months for maximum effect. And what an effect they had. Readers who fell in love with McGee in the *Deep Blue Good-by* got to see him grow and change along with the region and the country itself, all the way up to *The Lonely Silver Rain* in 1985.

That's a large part of the pleasure of this color-coded series. Throughout the books, McGee lives on a fifty-two-foot houseboat called the *Busted Flush*, which he won in a poker game. You don't have to be a diehard fan to know it's been docked at slip F-18 at the Bahia Mar Marina in Fort Lauderdale. (There's a plaque stating as much in the general location of that slip today.) We soon learn the man's eye and hair color, his age, his height and weight, his sense of honor. We feel, very soon, that we know *him*.

Deep Blue Good-by author, John D. MacDonald, wrote twenty-one books featuring his hero Travis McGee. *Wikimedia Commons.*

Most of all, we come to know his love of Florida. For anyone, native to the state or immigrant (MacDonald was the latter), who yearns for the good old days, Travis McGee understands. Back in 1964, he was already bemoaning the changes wrought by development and industry. Perhaps his biggest heartache is saved for the Everglades, but MacDonald waxes eloquent for his hero about the death by a thousand condos that takes over his beloved home throughout the years.

Why did he name each book in the series with a color? It could have been a gimmick. But starting with blue and ending with silver is also a rather profound metaphor for the maturation of a man along with his environment. When you put all these colors together, you get what you always get: *noir.*

FUN FACTS ABOUT THE *DEEP BLUE GOOD-BY*

MacDonald had originally considered naming McGee "Dallas," but since John F. Kennedy had recently been assassinated there, he didn't want to stir up bad associations. Eventually, he named his character after Travis Air Force Base in California. Also, several attempts have been made to film the novel, starting with Oliver Stone directing and Leonard DiCaprio as our hero. More recently, Christian Bale was slated for another go-around with director James Mangold, but due to a knee injury, the actor had to—bail.

Dexter

Novels by Jeff Lindsay

Dexter (2006-13)
Dexter: New Blood (2021-22)

TV Series Starring Michael C. Hall, Jennifer Carpenter, David Zayas, Christina Robinson and Desmond Harrington

TWO SIDES TO EVERY STORY

According to *Dexter* creator Jeff Lindsay, who wrote eight novels featuring the blood spatter analyst and serial killer—the first of which spawned the hit series—the only place his character could live besides Miami is Perth, Australia, which strikes him as a similar kind of place. Why these two cities? There's something about the juxtaposition of the palm trees and pastels of paradise against all those decapitated corpses. Something about the darkness that is the flip side of the stereotype of Miami's (and, presumably, Perth's) shallowness. The author seems to be saying that our antihero Dexter Morgan is a guy who, like these cities, feels empty.

Lindsay (real name Jeffry P. Freundlich), a Miami native who still lives in the state, is a true Floridian. Married to a niece of Key West denizen Ernest Hemingway, he has written sixteen books and two comics series, ten of which were based on the Dexter character. But while the opening tracking shot of the show's pilot definitely depicts Miami's South Beach—and the soundtrack is Latin music and the character's voiceover says that Miami is great and he loves Cuban food—the rest of the series is primarily filmed

Don't worry, serial killer Dexter Morgan, portrayed in the TV series by Michael C. Hall, kills (almost) only bad guys. *TCD/Prod.DB/Alamy Stock Photo.*

elsewhere, including in Los Angeles and Canada. In other words, there is deception at the show's very core. But then again, that's television. Come to think of it, that's also art. And often murder.

Deception. Two faces. Antihero. Dexter is the quintessential antihero, so anti, in fact, that CBS refused to air episodes during the 2007–8 television writer's strike despite the dearth of content because it did not wish to promote antisocial behavior. Maybe they had something there. Copycat cases from New Orleans to Norway have popped up with the "*Dexter* defense." That is to say, they modeled their behavior after you-know-who.

But that's just the "anti" part of antihero. Like any well-rounded character, Dexter's got some things going for him. Not only does he work for the fictional Miami Metro Police Department as a forensic analyst, but *he only kills bad guys!* At least that's his code—until he breaks it.

The interesting thing is, this guy is pretty self-aware. He knows full well that he's a fake; he says that he fakes human interactions very well. So well, in fact, that as his character develops throughout the run of the series, he actually falls in love and almost learns to act like a human being, a species with whom he has not previously identified.

All of which resonated with the public in spades. The series broke all sorts of records for Showtime viewership. It won Golden Globes for stars Michael

C. Hall and John Lithgow and many nominations. It earned, with one season's notable exception, good reviews. Apart from heavy-hitter Lithgow, it also attracted cast members like Jimmy Smits, Margo Martindale, JoBeth Williams, Edward James Olmos, Colin Hanks, Keith Carradine and Julia Stiles. And it ran for eight years, along with a brief comeback season.

In other words, it was a success. Maybe that's because, for all the deception, at least (like Miami and presumably Perth) Dexter knows who and what he is. After all, he named his boat *Slice of Life*. Ouch.

FUN FACTS ABOUT *DEXTER*

The general consensus about the third season of *Dexter* is that it's a dud and should be skipped. The fourth season is widely considered the best.

Done Deal (2012)

Novel by Les Standiford

STRIKE THREE

Baseball is to Miami like—what? There was a time when Major League teams only came to Florida in the off-season, a boon for snowbird Yankees who missed the national pastime. Known as the Grapefruit League (as opposed to Arizona's Cactus League), on the state's west coast alone, the Philadelphia Phillies have come to Clearwater since 1947, the Pittsburgh Pirates started coming to Bradenton in 1969 and the Toronto Blue Jays first came down to Dunedin in 1997. On the east coast, teams make the trip to Jupiter and West Palm. Today, fifteen Major League baseball teams still engage in the annual spring training ritual in Florida. Class A Advanced Florida State League teams and two Class AA teams play here as well.

Former Marlins player Destrade Orestes with fans. *State Archives of Florida.*

The state now boasts two Major League Florida teams of its own: the National League (East Division) Miami Marlins (since 1993, before which they were known as the Florida Marlins) and the American League (East Division) Tampa Bay Rays (1998). And baseball is, of course, big business. Well over $500 million pours into state coffers from spring training alone. Meanwhile, the Miami Marlins are worth approximately $1 billion and the Tampa Bay Rays about $25 million more.

In this first of his successful eight-book series of thrillers featuring John Deal, Les Standiford, the Florida International University creative writing program founding director, brings his reluctant hero into the path of an illegal plan to capitalize on Miami's plans for a Major League team of its own. The city is competing against others for the franchise, including two in Florida. Down on his luck, Deal, a former college ballplayer and current small-time building contractor in his family's failing business, is, at first, pretty enthusiastic about his hometown's latest venture. But when some scam artists start playing hardball with Deal's life—and his wife—his prospects quickly change. He has a decision to make, and suffice it to say, he doesn't sit this one out.

As things turn out, it all boils down to a property dispute. And property to Miami is like food for sharks.

Down and Out in the Magic Kingdom (2003)

Novel by Cory Doctorow

THE WORLD OF TOMORROW

The time is indeterminate, but we do know that this novel is set in "late XXI." The place is the Magic Kingdom in the Walt Disney World Resort, still located on twenty-five thousand acres in Lake Buena Vista, Florida, as it has been since 1971. Our antihero is Julius, who is only about one hundred years old, yet he is dating Lil, who is about 15 percent his age. Still, they have a lot in common. They have both lived and worked behind the scenes in the Magic Kingdom since the rise of the new world order, known as the Bitchun Society, and they share a fondness for the old ways, when people actually had human experiences. Now, trans-humans, who are part-machine, part-person, are everywhere, with implanted computers and wifi, cochlear telephones and the ability to (1) clone their bodies with a backup brain, (2) deadhead (or put themselves on hold for any amount of time) or (3) die, depending on their wishes. What's more, they can choose to look any age and make all kinds of upgrades to their skin, limbs, eyes, whatever. In this brave new world, doctors are merely technicians. And anyone can get a reboot at will.

Like the best sci-fi, *Down and Out* has lots of interesting ideas. The women, whatever their chronological age, still choose to appear in their twenties, while the men choose to appear about thirty years older. (Some things, Doctorow is telling us, never change.) Whuzzie is social capital—there is no actual money—which you can instantaneously keep track of for yourself and anyone you happen to meet. The more whuzzie you have, the more prestige you have and the more pleasure you can get out of a life that is, if you consider only food, housing and medical expenses, cost-free.

Despite the lack of need, however, there is still a lot of tension, in this instance, surrounding the drive to revamp the Haunted Mansion in the style of the Hall of Presidents. The

What would it be like to live and work at Disney World? *Down and Out in the Magic Kingdom* describes it. *Wikimedia Commons.*

Hall of Presidents has been renovated by a process called "flashbaking," which imprints the experience of the ride directly onto the guests' brains rather than having the animatronic presidents physically in front of them, like the good old days.

Which brings us to the heart of the book. Doctorow's novel, for all its clever, futuristic touches, makes a strong case for humanity that is directly in opposition to the whiz-bang innovations that created Disneyland and Disney World out of rural, flat land and cattle pastures in the first place. In what planet, in other words, is a robot Abe Lincoln natural? Is Doctorow telling us that Disney World has gone too far in the automation of Florida, indeed in the Disney-fication of the planet? Or have they gotten it just right and should now stop fixing what ain't broke?

Recently, Disney World, which for years enjoyed deep tax breaks from the state, has been at loggerheads with the governor, whose social views lean much farther right than those of the company. This means that it has lost the ability to effectively tax and govern itself, a sweetheart of a sweetheart deal that it has enjoyed for decades. Although the situation appears to be improving, Disney's special protected status is certainly a thing of the past.

So much for the World of Tomorrow.

Fear Thy Neighbor (2022)

Novel by Fern Michaels

CULT ISLAND

Bestselling novelist Fern Michaels combines mystery, mayhem, romance and the strong or broken bonds between parents and children in this latest addition to her one-hundred-plus book output. And this time, her setting is a fictional Southwest Florida island—based on a real one—that is both heartbreakingly beautiful and extremely unsettling to a scarred young woman.

When Michaels's twenty-nine-year-old heroine, Alison, finds herself in the fictional Southwest Florida city of Fort Charlotte and then on nearby Palmetto Island, she has no idea that she is stumbling into a story that dates back over a century. Traumatized from a childhood of bad foster homes in Ohio, Ali wears her anger and suspicion like a cage—nothing can come too close. The very beach house she decides, on a whim, to purchase turns out to be the burial site of human bones—and the subject of a mysterious rumor that has been haunting the island for years. In the process of discovering the truth about her new home, Ali meets some very sweet and some extremely disturbing locals.

There really is a *Port* Charlotte, just forty miles away from Estero Island, the place that served as headquarters for a cult in the late eighteenth and early nineteenth centuries. The closest city to the island is actually Fort Myers; Estero is located in Fort Myers Beach.

The book's reference to an unnamed religious utopian community in fact points to the very real, if defunct, Koreshan Unity. The group was founded by a Dr. Cyrus (Koresh in Persian) Teed from Upstate New York in the 1870s, who aimed to mesh religion with science at a time when the two were very much at odds. Teed, who received the Florida property from a wealthy follower, claimed that God had come to him in a vision to say that the Earth is a hollow ball that contains the entire universe, with the sun at its core. His flock came to believe in reincarnation, as well as a God that was at once male and female. The Koreshans, as they were called, lived on a 320-acre plot in Estero, which Teed earmarked for his "New Jerusalem." When he failed to return from the dead after his demise in 1908, the group began to disband.

The strange goings-on in the book may or may not have anything to do with the actual cult. Still, the story is a reminder that, like the bones, the past is rarely buried deeply enough to not be unearthed.

FUN FACT ABOUT *FEAR THY NEIGHBOR*

Henry Ford was an early enthusiast, if not a devotee, of the Koreshans. Also, the Koreshan land is now the two-hundred-acre Koreshan State Historic Site, with all the amenities, from nature trails and fishing spots to boat rentals and a farmers' market. David Koresh (née Vernon Wayne Howell), the leader of the Branch Davidians and the central figure in the 1993 siege in Waco, Texas, used the name for the same reason Teed translated his: Koresh was the Persian name of King Cyrus, who allowed the Jews in Babylon to return to Israel.

The Flamingo Feather (1887)

Novel by Kirk Munroe

A NEW WORLD FRIENDSHIP

In the early 1560s, the teenaged nephew of French Huguenot explorer René Goulaine de Laudonnière is orphaned, and he makes his way to his uncle in Paris, who takes him on the adventure of a lifetime: a voyage to the Great River of May (now known as the St. Johns River) near present-day Jacksonville. The goal: help establish New France in the New World.

The true story of naval officer Jean Ribault, the sacking of Fort Caroline (which the victorious Spanish renamed Fort San Mateo) and the rivalry between the French and the Spanish in the New World—St. Augustine, incidentally, was founded in 1565—has been told many times, but perhaps never as well as it is in this brief novel, written by Kirk Munroe in 1887. In it, that fictional nephew, Rene de Veaux, forges a deep friendship with Has-se, the son of a great Timucuan chief, which helps save both French and Native lives. But sadly, it did not help the French settlement, which quickly fell to the Spanish, ably aided by the Seminoles. Today, no trace of the fort remains, and its exact location is unknown. Yet a national memorial to the failed French colony stands on the approximate site in the Timucuan Ecological and Historic Preserve.

That striking flamingo feather, meanwhile, is worn in the novel as a headpiece by the son of the chief, and Has-se gives one to De Veaux as a sign of their deep friendship. (Later, the young white man earns it.) These wading birds, of course, have long been a familiar image in Florida, never more so than when the real ones were decimated by hunters in search of adornments for ladies' hats. While the live adults can stand five feet tall or more, tiny replicas show up everywhere from Christmas decorations to cocktail straws and, of course, lotto tickets. Flamingo-named businesses dot the landscape, as do towns, like Flamingo, in Monroe County. What is it about the gorgeously gawky creature that so entices? Something about the salmon pink feathers and black beak, plus those long legs that are to die for, all connected to a body that weighs about six pounds. Recently, the debate about whether flamingos should be deemed a threatened species has been mitigated by a healthy number of pink visitors that arrived with Hurricane Idalia in 2023, and so far, fingers crossed, they have hung around.

When the historical events in *The Flamingo Feather* occurred, the birds were far more plentiful. *Wikimedia Commons.*

A note to readers: Writing in 1887, Munroe, the author of *Wakulla* and other books, used a curious elevated diction ("thee" and "thou") for his dialogue. More disturbing to many readers are the epithets "simple-minded" and "savage" used for the Natives. On the other hand, the plot greatly honors the Natives. So, it's a toss-up.

FUN FACT ABOUT FLAMINGOES

A group of them is called a *flamboyance.*

Flipper (1963)

Film Directed by James B. Clark; Starring Chuck Connors, Luke Halpin, Joe Higgins and Kathleen Maguire

Flipper's New Adventure (1964)

Film Directed by Leon Benson; Starring Luke Halpin, Tom Helmore and Brian Kelly

Flipper (1964-67)

TV Series Starring Brian Kelly, Luke Halpin, Burt Reynolds, Tommy Norden and Andy Devine

Flipper (1995-2000)

TV Series Also Known as *Flipper: The New Adventures*; Starring Jessica Alba, Payton Haas, Colleen Flynn and Brian Wimmer

Flipper (1996)

Film Directed by Alan Shapiro; Starring Paul Hogan, Elijah Wood, Chelsea Field and Isaac Hayes

MAKE WAY FOR DOLPHINS

The Florida-based entertainment franchise that was *Flipper* began with the story of a young Key West boy who neglects his chores after adopting an injured dolphin despite his fisherman father's better judgment. If this sounds like the South Florida, waterlogged version of *The Yearling*, you might be onto something, although legendary stunt diver and underwater photographer Ricou Browning actually got the idea while watching his kids inhale episodes of *Lassie*. Not that it makes a difference. The formula is a great one, and it clearly aced the transition from deer and dog to marine mammal. Think of all those spectacular underwater shots. Think of teenybopper heartthrob Luke Halpin shirtless. And think of legendary Florida filmmaker (*Daktari, Sea Hunt,* etc.) Ivan Tors, who produced the movie that was shot at his eponymous Miami-based studio.

Although the Florida locations are renamed, the Keys have a long commercial history with Atlantic bottlenose dolphins. In 1946, the marine mammal park Theater of the Sea, now well known for allowing tourists to swim with these amazing creatures, took up residence in Islamorada, on

Not all bottlenose dolphins are as intelligent as those that appeared in *Flipper*, but many come close. *Wikimedia Commons*.

Windley Key. The species is a great choice for an animal act, possessing unusual intelligence and sociability. They also communicate through sound, particularly through squeals and whistles. Dolphins are a staple of the Miami Seaquarium, SeaWorld in Orlando and other Florida marine attractions.

But let's return to the ailing dolphin. Theater of the Sea in Islamorada is a haven for marine animals that cannot be released into the wild for numerous reasons, including serious injuries from ingesting seemingly innocuous trash, like plastic six-pack holders. The more these creatures interact with human beings—which, ironically, *Flipper* popularized—the most vulnerable they are to harm. The point of *Flipper* was not for kids to try this at home. It was for everyone to recognize the dignity and beauty of our natural world.

FUN FACTS ABOUT *FLIPPER*

The dolphin that originally played Flipper was an animal actor named Mitzi, who lived from 1958 to 1972. In that and subsequent iterations of the franchise, other females—who tend to be more sociable than males—played the dolphin, sometimes several at a time. But few could reproduce Mitzi's signature tail walk. Also, one of the five main Flipper dolphins, Susie, actually saved producer Ivan Tors's life in the water. What's more, Flipper's distinctive voice was actually the engineered call of a kookaburra, a native bird of Australia and New Guinea.

Florida (2018)

Stories by Lauren Groff

BLOOD, SWEAT OR TEARS

Far from the tourists, the Mouse and the beaches, the men, women and children of Gainesville resident Lauren Groff's story collection *Florida* have all they can do just to keep on keeping on. In the first tale, a Florida writer prowls the streets of her neighborhood every night and then takes her young sons to France for a month, ostensibly to research a book about the extremely famous, albeit immensely misogynistic, late author Guy de Maupassant. Her goal: to escape not just the heat, but also the humanity, specifically her loving, hardworking husband. In another story, two young sisters are abandoned by their parents and forced to exist on their wits in a wild and isolated encampment. Groff fills her stories with houses by swamps teeming with snakes and sinkholes and properties overgrown with palmettos, vines and, of course, bugs. So many bugs. We encounter ghosts and hurricanes, panthers lurking in the dark, a household accident and men who either appear more dangerous than they are or are more dangerous than they appear.

Goff's heroines—because the stories are mainly female-centered—are educated and solidly middle class, but even that doesn't save them from existential despair. In one of her most chilling stories, "Above and Below," a grad student finds herself homeless and alone after losing her funding. She may have resources among both family and friends. A college graduate, she should be able to find a job. But Groff seems to be telling us that although the skies are often clear and the living is supposedly easy, no one escapes Florida, or life, for that matter, unscathed. She recognizes what the tourist council won't tell the northerners who flee to the South for a lifelong vacation: whoever you are, you take that with you wherever you go—even to Florida.

FUN FACT ABOUT *FLORIDA*

The book was a finalist for the National Book Award for Fiction in 2018. It did win the Story Prize, awarded to collections of short fiction.

Florida Man (2023)

TV Series Created by Donald Todd; Starring Edgar Ramirez, Abbey Lee, Anthony LaPaglia, Otmara Marrero and Emory Cohen

WHEREVER YOU GO, YOU'RE THERE

Drug-crazed Florida man steals ambulance and winds up in front of sheriff's office operations center, where he is promptly arrested. Florida man is crushed to death in porta-potty by bulldozer driven by coworker. These are not mere plot devices in a goofy series; they are true events that have made headlines in Florida and contributed to the meme of the laughably stupid titular troublemaker. But yes, the writers did riff on them for this absurdist, seven-episode comedy-thriller.

Coproduced by Jason Bateman of *Ozark* and *Arrested Development* fame, *Florida Man* is the story of Mike Valentine, a Latino Florida native who hightailed it away from his corrupt police chief father and disturbing family dynamics to start fresh in Philadelphia. (If you're thinking it's usually the other way around, you've got a point.) But—big surprise—things don't go as planned. The action starts with Mike fighting back tears to tell his Gamblers Anonymous meeting that he lost his job, his friends and his wife. Turns out, he's a former cop who now serves as an enforcer for a mobster (he terrorizes other gamblers to pay their debts). When his boss sends him back to Florida to find his runaway girlfriend—she is in fact a girlfriend to *both* of them, but don't tell the mobster—he winds up in his fictional hometown of Coronado Beach, not far from the very real Disney World in Lake Buena Vista, outside of Orlando.

Florida Man is not for the faint of heart. But the tone, even when the action is gruesome, is usually light, much like another Florida-set thriller, *Burn Notice*. In the first installment alone, there is a chase scene in a hardware store, a graphically broken leg, a lot of blood that may or may not be real, a shark bite in the groin and prescient wisdom from dear old dad to the effect that a man can change his location, but wherever he goes, he takes himself with him. While that is a good insight, the show could never have been called "Philadelphia Man."

So, what is it about Florida that inspired the Florida man meme, first recognized in 2013 on Reddit and Tumblr? A fair amount of drugs and just enough money? A macho culture? Ira P. Robbins wrote a *Florida State University Law Review* paper in which he noted that although some claim it's the state's Public Records Law, which emphasizes government transparency and leads to some of the most long-lived internet memes, this is actually not the case. People just like to joke about the weird behavior of Floridians.

Personally, I blame it on the heat and humanity. *You* try to think clearly when you're dripping wet half the time.

FUN FACT ABOUT *FLORIDA MAN*

The show was actually filmed in Wilmington, North Carolina.

The Florida Project (2017)

Film Directed by Sean Baker; Starring Brooklynn Prince, Willem Dafoe and Bria Vinaite

THE TRAGIC KINGDOM

In a couple of thirty-five-dollar-a-night Kississimee motels within spitting distance—and in this movie, you can take the word *spit* literally—from Walt Disney World, live a not-so-free spirit named Halley; her six-year-old daughter, Moonee; and a number of other down-and-out characters you don't normally see in American feature films. We first meet Moonee and her little friends expectorating down from their balconies onto the windshields of other guests' cars. It's not only a foreshadowing of the children's ongoing behavior, but it's also a perfect metaphor for the way the rest of the world views them and their parents.

For all its sun-soaked color and adorable children, *Project* is a painful movie to watch. Even if you don't see the irony of a sad transient motel called The Magic Castle or the film's title, which might as well refer to a housing project, the message is clear. Plenty of families in the Orlando area and beyond cannot subsist on the low wages they earn for serving well-heeled tourists. And while Baker is by no means shooting a documentary, he might as well be. There really is a Magic Castle Inn and Suites. Six miles from the theme park on U.S. Highway 192, it sits ready for any tourist (ironies abound here) who wants to explore Halley and Moonee's home in room 323. And there really are plenty of people who exist from paycheck to paycheck in places they should not inhabit long term, thanks to the kindness of those like the fictional manager Bobby, a man, played by the peerless Willem Dafoe, who is trying to show mercy within a merciless system.

The Florida Project was shot on a miniscule budget by Hollywood standards of just $2 million. It earned well over five times that, and Dafoe was nominated for an Oscar while he and the film earned nods for many other awards. Vinaite and Prince were also widely praised, and the flick made the lists of the American Film Institute's and the National Film Board's top ten movies of the year.

But have you heard of it? Did you see it? Chances are good that you haven't. It's not just the view of a shattered American dream—or the painful scenes of a mother who entertains strange men in the bedroom while her child holes up in the bathtub—that kept many people away. Disney World looms huge in the Florida psyche; it's so powerful that it actually has a prohibited air zone 365 days a year that the moviemakers could not afford. Not long ago, it was the most popular vacation resort in the world, boasting nearly $60 million in annual ticket sales.

That means a lot of pride and season passes for Florida residents. It means a lot of money for the state. I don't mean to be paranoid here. I'm just suggesting that most of us are not too anxious to mess with the mouse.

FUN FACTS ABOUT *THE FLORIDA PROJECT*

The Florida Project was the working title the Disney Corporation called the land on which Disney World was built when it was still in the planning stages. Also, helicopters were not supposed to fly overhead during the movie, but the budget did not allow for them to be rerouted. So, the script was changed to accommodate them. What's more, the director found the actress Bria Vinaite, who played Halley, on Instagram.

Florida Roadkill (1999)

Novel by Tim Dorsey

LAUGHING ALL THE WAY TO THE MORGUE

Tim Dorsey was certainly not the first author—nor the last—to mix homicide with hilarity, but he was hands down one of the best. While most of the former *Tampa Tribune* reporter's dozens of crime novels feature Serge A. Storms, a character who gives new meaning to the term *antihero*, they are all terrifically written romps, with memorable lines such as "the polyp of land that dangles into Tampa Bay like a uvula" and casts of characters a reader would never want to meet in a dark alley. Or on a sun-drenched beach. Or, for that matter, at an AA meeting.

Dorsey's subgenre has been called Sunbelt Baroque. In his case, the violence is notably bizarro but still manages to deliver a gut punch. One man is murdered with a pair of shrinking jeans, another with inverted alcohol poisoning and a third may be the only case in literature of death by "Fix a Flat." A dentist's insured hands are destroyed with a chainsaw by our psychopathic heroes. And let's not forget the unusual use that Dorsey finds for a convenience store hot dog skewer.

This kind of book certainly may not be everybody's cup of tea, particularly when laughs are squeezed out of a young beauty's devastating drug habit. But most reviewers of Dorsey's work, which ended with *The Maltese Iguana* before his untimely death in late 2023 at the age of sixty-two, entirely miss the point. They don't realize that Dorsey's nutjob Storms is also a nut about Florida. After all, Dorsey was a reporter. Besides the usual nods to the Marlins, the Miami drug scene and Tarpon Springs spongers, he can wax eloquent on everything from the founding of Tampa to Teddy Roosevelt and his Rough Riders, key deer and on-location movie shoots of Peter Fonda movies. In other words, there's an entire education about the state to be found between the murders in these goofy, horrifying stories. And of all people to teach it, a homicidal maniac scam artist may be the most interesting.

Like life, Dorsey seems to be telling readers, Florida is full of surprises. Trust nobody. Take nothing at face value. And look for beauty, meaning and knowledge wherever you find it. It's a fascinating lesson to glean from such ugliness.

Laugh and learn.

FUN FACTS ABOUT *FLORIDA ROADKILL*

Unlike the second banana in most crime duos, Serge A. Storm's sidekick was a stoner named Coleman. By the way, author Tim Dorsey was incredibly prolific. He published his twenty-six books in just twenty-four years.

Florida Woman (2022)

Novel by Deb Rogers

MONKEY BUSINESS

Nature has a well-deserved reputation when it comes to rehabilitation. In this debut novel, a twenty-seven-year-old felon named Jamie is offered a summer under house arrest at the fictional Atlas Wildlife Refuge, which abuts the Ocala National Forest in Central Florida. Despite the ferocious heat and mosquitoes, for a while, she can't quite believe her luck. The grounds are pristine, the sunsets a delight. Plus, the compound houses dozens of macaques, primates originally from Asia, Europe and North Africa that have been saved from experimentation or other abuse. Our heroine quickly befriends the animals. Best of all, the three female human residents are extraordinarily sincere, spiritual and welcoming. They seem to delight in everything about Jamie, especially her video skills, because they are desperate to enhance their web presence to increase donations. For the first time in her difficult and lonely life, Jamie seriously considers laying down roots—until, that is, it all goes horribly wrong.

"Florida man" is a meme that refers to a certain type of news report about bizarre, foolhardy behavior that is invariably printed under a headline that begins with those two words. (Think "Florida Man Loses Arm in Soda Machine" or "Florida Man Leaves ID Behind in Bank Heist.") This novel turns the meme on its head. It is a deadly serious thriller that pits a lost and, yes, foolish woman (her crime, which involved her employer's bar, stolen dollar bills, a fire and a pelican, was caught on a security video that went viral)

Feral macaques are a serious problem in some parts of Florida. *Wikimedia Commons*.

against a coven of the-ends-justify-the-means cultists. And it all takes place against a magnificently realized Florida forest backdrop that oozes danger and beauty in equal portions.

The problem of non-native, feral macaques in Florida that the book addresses is massive. Apparently, the monkey known as the rhesus macaque was released on a river island south of Gainesville by a commercial river boat captain in a bid to boost tourism. The troop swam to the nearby forest, and the rest is a matter of monkey see, monkey do—not to mention birds and bees. Others in the Keys and Titusville are the sad survivors of a breeding lab and amusement park and their offspring. What's more, the Florida Fish and Wildlife Conservation Commission states that not only do many of these primates have rabies, but every single one also carries the potentially fatal herpes B virus.

So, maybe nature isn't quite so rehabilitative after all. But who wants to spoil a good suspense novel?

Free Ride (2013)

Film Directed by Shana Betz; Starring Anna Paquin, Drea de Matteo, Cam Gigandet and Liana Liberato

MOTHER MAY NOT ALWAYS KNOW BEST

Say it's 1977, and you're an attractive single mom of two in Barberton, Ohio, who's just gotten badly beaten up by your boyfriend. Your mother's a pain, your factory job is going nowhere and your fifteen-year-old has a mouth on her like you haven't heard since you were fifteen. So, you call your girlfriend in Fort Lauderdale, and before you know it, you're picking your kids up from school with the car all packed and pointed southeast.

Or maybe you're the teenager, who's just made a date to meet a bad boy after the final bell when your mother pulls up and, to your fury, announces that if you're not prepared to take the map and navigate, you can get out of the car, and she and your sister will leave you behind.

But what if you're the second daughter? The sweet little girl who's been watching your big sister grow up and your mother get knocked around? And you're excited as can be to get to Florida—until you find out what's actually in store for you?

You make this movie.

Based on Shana Betz's own experience, *Free Ride* gives viewers a front-row seat to the challenges faced by a young blue-collar worker who is fiercely devoted to her children and will do anything to take care of them, even if it requires a little drug smuggling. OK, a lot of drug smuggling. And the irony is not lost on Betz, whose alter ego says to her mother and sister their first night on the road before the three bed down in the car, "Good night, John Boy." That ode to *The Waltons*, the ultimate old-fashioned 1970s family drama, underscores the difficulty of making ends meet the old-fashioned way.

Back in the 1970s, before the ultra-hipness of Miami and the all-out commercialism of Disney, Florida's reputation was based largely on its status as a retirement haven. Out-of-staters didn't recognize that, as in any state, many transplants and natives were actually under the age of eighteen. (Some say that given the state of Florida's public education system, longtime taxpayers don't always recognize the fact themselves.) In this movie, characters actually wear uniforms to go to public school. Plus, they do their homework—or at least they say they did. Some things never change.

Gentle Giant (1967)

Film Directed by James Neilson; Starring Clint Howard, Dennis Weaver and Vera Miles

Gentle Ben (1967–69)

TV Series Starring Clint Howard, Dennis Weaver and Beth Brickell

THE BEARLING

Here's an original concept: a young boy befriends a wild orphaned animal in Florida and grows up alongside it. If you're thinking of *The Yearling* or *Flipper*, that's not your fault. Although the novel on which the Gentle Ben franchise was based is in fact set in Alaska, the adaptations of the story, set in the Everglades at least in part to use producer Ivan Tors's (of *Sea Hunt*, *Flipper* and *Daktari* fame) Miami production studio, otherwise appear mighty familiar to anyone with a passing knowledge of Marjorie Kinnan Rawlings's masterpiece. And that's OK. Because the more asphalt and concrete that got spread around these parts and the more the Everglades was ravaged, the more important it was to remember the critters who were here long before the rest of us.

In the Walt Morey children's novel, a lonely Alaskan teenager named Mark Anderson forms a relationship with a captive adult brown bear (kids, don't try this at home) and ultimately saves its life. On the heels of the book came the 1967 film *Gentle Giant*, in which the Wedloe family lives near a game reserve in Florida when young Mark Wedloe befriends a black bear cub. Poachers shoot the mother and pluck up the cub, and Mark reports

In *Gentle Giant* and *Gentle Ben*, Clint Howard befriends a brown bear played by several like these. *State Archives of Florida/Florida-Division of Tourism.*

them to the authorities, leading to a revenge plot. Not to worry: Dad, who had been a pilot spotting fish for locals, becomes a wildlife officer in the Glades, and boy and bear are reunited. The hit TV series continues the Wedloe saga, with Ben now weighing in at about seven hundred pounds. There was also an animated series and two made-for-TV movies.

To be sure, there were many who objected to the obvious dangers of portraying a small boy hanging out with a bear (the country of Sweden and the U.S. National Park Service for starters). But hey, this is fantasy. And for my money, it's better than depicting adults poaching these animals. Although perhaps in both cases, *Gentle Ben* works as a cautionary tale to not only let sleeping bears lie but also respect the natural environment—Florida's in particular.

FUN FACTS ABOUT *GENTLE GIANT* AND *GENTLE BEN*

Eight-year-old Clint Howard (Ron's brother) was never hurt by Bruno the bear, who played Ben in the film and most of the time in the series. However, the child actor once needed help when his ursine costar chose to sit on him. Also, different bears were filmed for different bear skills. When Bruno needed to swim, run or fight, he had a stand-in.

The Glades (2010-13)

TV Series Created by Clifton Campbell; Starring
Matt Passmore, Kiele Sanchez, Carlos Gómez
and Jordan Wall

CRIME IN THE SWAMP

When Chicago homicide detective Jim Longworth gets shot in the rear end by his boss due to the captain's mistaken belief that he is sleeping with his wife, the aggrieved cop is in for a major payday. Being too young, cocky and good-looking for retirement, he decides to give himself a sort of working vacation by joining the Florida Department of Law Enforcement. He will, he figures, live happily ever after in paradise. Play a few rounds of golf. Work on his tan. Catch a jaywalker or two. The good life awaits!

Wait. This guy is supposed to be smart?

It's not quite *Miami Vice*. Yet this fairly old-school police procedural ran for four seasons and broke its network's ratings record for an original drama series, with as many as 3.6 million viewers per episode. When the network unexpectedly pulled the plug after the season four cliffhanger finale—due, presumably, to the waning of those ratings—millions woke up one morning to the realization that they would never learn who shot Jim Longworth a second time. Although they could be fairly certain that, had there been another season, the main character would have survived the hit.

The show makes good use of its locations, such as the season two opener on Calle Ocho, the heart of Latino Miami. What's more, the fictional Palm Glades in South Florida does look authentic. More to the point, the premise that a northerner would consider a stressful job in the Miami area as a

This fella could have been an extra in *The Glades*. *Wikimedia Commons.*

vacation is really not so far-fetched. Plenty of tourists come down for a few weeks of pleasure and piña coladas. They learn that Floridians pay no state income tax. They see no snow. So, they relocate. When they move here, however, they are faced with bumper-to-bumper rush hour traffic on I-95, crime, sea lice in the ocean and hurricanes on the shore. Not to mention the same daily annoyances they left behind.

And when they come to the realization that there's no escaping the very things that make life a challenge up north, it might even lead to murder.

FUN FACT ABOUT *THE GLADES*

The show was originally supposed to be set in the Tampa Bay area with the title "Sugarloaf." Also, the interior shots were filmed in a warehouse in Broward County, not far from Fort Lauderdale.

The Golden Girls (1985-92)

TV Series Created by Susan Harris; Starring Bea Arthur, Estelle Getty, Rue McClanahan and Betty White

MIAMI NOT-ALWAYS-SO-NICE

Bad blood between actors in an ensemble cast. Slut-shaming. Mocking a star's appearance. Incipient dementia. Racist tropes.

For a sitcom that was originally conceived as "Miami Nice," the CBS mega-hit known as *The Golden Girls* was, at times, anything but. Its seven seasons and 180 episodes presented more than their share of bad feelings, both on and off screen. Pretty interesting for a show with the theme song "Thank You for Being a Friend."

The concept was simple: three widows—two in their sixties, one eighty—and the eighty-year-old's fifty-five-year-old divorcée daughter share a home in Miami. One widow is a Southern sexpot. Another is an airheaded farm girl. The eldest is a tough-talking Italian, and her daughter is intelligent, touchy and relatively unattractive.

What could possibly go wrong?

For one thing, Bea Arthur (Dorothy Zbornak) and costar Betty White (Rose Nylund) did not always get along. They worked together fine, but their personalities and acting styles led to ongoing tension off set.

Rue McClanahan's Blanche Devereaux was the butt—excuse the expression—of hundreds of jokes about her promiscuity at the height of the AIDS crisis, which, interestingly, was addressed and handled sensitively on the show.

Betty White, Bea Arthur, Rue McClanahan and Estelle Getty shine in *The Golden Girls*. *United Archives GmbH/Alamy Stock Photo.*

Bea Arthur threatened to quit if the jokes about her character's appearance were not toned down. They were. Nevertheless, the show folded when she decided to leave, and the short-lived *Golden Palace* spin-off never spun far.

Estelle Getty, who began her role as eighty-year-old Sophia Petrillo at the age of sixty-two, suffered from stage fright that was so crippling, it, along with the onset of dementia, made it difficult for her to learn her lines. She eventually resorted to using cue cards.

Then there was the interracial marriage episode in which Blanche and Rose wore mud masks, claiming, "We're not Black," which caused Hulu to temporarily pull the episode off the air in reruns.

On the plus side, all four lead actresses won Primetime Emmys; the show, which was in Nielsen's top ten for six of its seven years, was also in the TV Guide's list of the sixty best series of all times. It won two Primetime Emmys for outstanding comedy series and three Golden Globes for best television series (musical or comedy). It tackled important issues of its time, especially those facing seniors, including death and assisted suicide, eldercare, age discrimination, poor medical care and poverty.

In other words, a blue-haired *Sex in the City* it wasn't.

FUN FACTS ABOUT *THE GOLDEN GIRLS*

The Tony-winning Broadway legend Elaine Stritch failed her audition for the part of Dorothy. Speaking of Dorothy, Bea Arthur hated the cheesecake the four women often indulged in during dessert strategy sessions. What's more, Arthur was actually a year older than her fictional mom Estelle Getty, who spent three hours in makeup to achieve the look of someone more than a decade and a half older than her true age. And what would you think if Betty White and Rue McClanahan swapped roles? It was actually considered.

Goldens Are Here (2018)

Novel by Andrew Furman

The year is 1961, and the place is Florida, specifically the Titusville/ Melbourne/Cape Canaveral area of Brevard County, around the Indian River, in what is now known as the Space Coast. It was a time when I-95 did not yet link Jacksonville in the north to Miami in the south. Disney World was still on the drawing board. Women left their babies in strollers outside stores.

But this is not *I Dream of Jeannie* territory. This is the land of small-time orange growers, of centuries-old racism, of labor unrest and of insistence on—and resistance to—change. First, the oranges. Ambersweet. Valencia. Hamlin. Navel. Temple. Thanks in part to the state's sandy soil and subtropical climate, including plenty of both sun and rain, the Florida Native tribes did well with the seeds they received from the Spanish in the early sixteenth century. An "orange rush" developed after the Civil War, with small growers clustering mainly along the St. Johns and Indian Rivers and in the "Golden Triangle" region of Mount Dora, Eustis and Tavares.

"In part" refers, of course, to promotion and marketing. Towns sprang up with names like Orange Springs (1850s), Orange City (1882) and Orange Lake (1926). Since 1909, the supremely fragrant orange blossom has been the state flower; for more than a quarter of a century, the fruit's image has appeared on state license plates, and it became the state fruit in 2005. Frozen concentrate, developed for soldiers during World War II, exploded in popularity with thrifty housewives in the postwar years—to the chagrin of small growers, who could not compete with the likes of Minute Maid. And although the citrus industry is no longer what it once was due to a twenty-year blight of "citrus greening disease," the $6.5 billion industry still boasts two thousand growers statewide. Climate change, particularly in the form of major hurricanes, is only adding to the crisis.

Oranges are like gold in *Goldens Are Here*. *Wikimedia Commons*.

The politics of orange growing is not what interests Isaac Golden, a fish-out-of-water Jewish Yankee who scoops up some prime land in order to both add to his co-op's yield and experiment with new varieties. An idealist, Isaac has a lot on his plate: a beautiful wife with a wandering eye, a young son with a rare genetic disorder, a needy toddler and the prying eyes and wagging tongues of old-time growers who just don't get him or like him much. Add to that antisemitic slurs carved into his trees and a Black labor organizer stirring up the pickers at harvest time, and the tension is palpable.

So is the history. Furman, a Florida Atlantic University English professor, puts readers in the mindset—as well as the environment—of small-town postwar southern life. The nation is changing; corporations are threatening to swallow small businessmen. The push for equal rights for not only Black Americans but also Jewish Americans is just a few years away. For some people, it's the good old days. For others, it's a launching pad.

FUN FACT ABOUT *GOLDENS ARE HERE*

The book's title refers to the hand-painted business sign on Melody Golden's fruit stand. It confuses prospective customers, who think "golden" is a variety of orange. In fact, there is a good-sized produce market called "Robert Is Here" in Homestead, which was the original sign the then-six-year-old proprietor Robert Moehling put on his childhood stand to sell his father's cucumbers at the same location.

Hoot (2006)

Film Directed by Wil Shriner; Starring Luke Wilson,
Logan Lerman, Brie Larson and Tim Blake Nelson

A BIRD IN THE HOLE

Realizing that his siblings' kids couldn't read his satirical bestselling crime novels, legendary Ft. Lauderdale native Carl Hiaasen wrote *Hoot* for the nine-to twelve-year-old set. The beloved former *Miami Herald* reporter's award-winning novel was subsequently turned into a movie that just barely, with the help of video sales but very little from critics, recovered its initial investment. Both the book and the movie make strong cases for environmentalism and against rampant development, but it's not hard to see why the movie, at least, was a disappointment.

Hiassen's previous film outing, *Striptease*, was commercially successful, thanks in large part to Demi Moore's nude scenes. But his razor-sharp prose, over-the-top characters and crazy situations don't seem to translate so well to the silver screen. Before the story is over, three activist middle schoolers in coastal "Coconut Cove," Florida, have lied, connived, vandalized a police car, harassed one adult with venomous cottonmouth snakes and bound and gagged another, fled a police officer—and never really suffered any consequences.

In fact, they end up heroes, with the bad guy in jail. That's because despite the shenanigans, *Hoot* does have heart. An evil regional manager plans to plant a Mother Paula's Pancake House smack dab over an endangered burrowing owl habitat. But it won't happen on the watch of these kids, one of whom actually stands in the path of a bulldozer. He isn't hurt, but activism doesn't come cheap. The teen who braved the bulldozer is bitten by guard dogs. And golfers accidentally conk out another one—twice. (The golf scenes were filmed in Key Largo's ritzy Ocean Reef Club.)

Those tiny burrowing owls are in fact protected under the Federal Migrating Bird Treaty Act. They are classified "state threatened" by the Florida Fish and Wildlife Conservation Commission. There are all sorts of rules about development in their habitat, which the fictional regional manager, incidentally, tears out of the regulations book. Along with sea turtles, they are among the most beloved of the state's fauna.

It's an argument the story makes well, as our middle school hero Roy Eberhardt encourages the crowd, which he and his friends have assembled under false pretenses, to stay silent for a full minute so as not to frighten the creatures from leaving their holes. One by one, those adorable little heads and bodies pop out of the ground, to the delight of everyone except the bad guy. Thankfully, the crowd likes them even better than pancakes. The by-now angry actress who plays Mother Paula spontaneously tells the assembled citizens and press that the company is donating the land for an owl sanctuary. And almost everyone, except for the arrested manager, lives happily ever after. Ah, if it were only so easy.

It's an important environmental lesson for both kids and adults—as long as they don't go about things quite the same way.

FUN FACT ABOUT *HOOT*

In one of several film cameos over the course of his long career, another beloved Florida artist, the late Key West balladeer Jimmy Buffett, figures prominently in the movie. Not only did he play Roy's kindly science teacher—in shorts, of course—but he also wrote and/or performed half a dozen of the movie's songs.

I Dream of Jeannie (1965-70)

TV Series Created by Sidney Sheldon;
Starring Barbara Eden, Larry Hagman and Bill Daily

OUT OF THE BOTTLE

Who cares if *I Dream of Jeannie* didn't make it into all those encyclopedias of the greatest American TV shows of all time? What does it matter that it was actually shot in and around Los Angeles, with only two cast-and-crew trips to Florida's Space Coast, where it was supposedly set? The well-loved sitcom, created by that mega-mogul of schlock Sidney Sheldon as NBC's answer to the wildly successful *Bewitched*, celebrated the Kennedy Space Center and the excitement and adventure of manned U.S. space flight in the way this country does best: with fantasy, sexual innuendo (remember that gorgeous midriff?) and a few cheap laughs. All meshed perfectly with the space-age Florida setting.

Larry Hagman and Barbara Eden barely set foot in Florida for the filming of *I Dream of Jeannie*. *Allstar Picture Library Limited/Alamy Stock Photo.*

Major Tony Nelson, played by Larry Hagman (who, in the subsequent decade, put the city of Dallas on the map with *that* memorable series), finds Jeannie's bottle (get it? Genie?) after mistakenly landing his spacecraft off the coast of a deserted island in the South Pacific. The astronaut inadvertently takes Jeannie and her bottle back home to 1020 Palm Drive in Cocoa Beach, where she proceeds to get him into all kinds of adorable trouble in her efforts to be his loving, if more than a little cuckoo, mate. Wait! What if anyone at the space center besides Nelson's daffy best friend, Roger Healey, were to learn about Jeannie's true identity or, worse, were to think that Nelson was too crazy to be a NASA employee? Suffice it to say, the work that went into the Mercury, Gemini and Apollo space programs was nothing compared to the machinations of Nelson and Healey in each twenty-five-minute episode.

Nutty, yes. But the combination of glamour, humor, American ingenuity and the sheer possibility and promise that was Florida, the United States and space flight in the 1960s made the show so popular that it spawned years of syndication and even two reunion films. When you think about it, it could break your heart—that is, if it weren't so silly.

FUN FACTS ABOUT *I DREAM OF JEANNIE*

In 1996, the Kennedy Space Center brought in Barbara Eden to speak at its Space Day event. In her honor, a small street in the area was renamed "I Dream of Jeannie Lane." Also, Jeannie's "genie in a bottle" home was in fact a special Christmas-edition Jim Beam bourbon bottle from 1964. Its exact origins on the set are the stuff of legend.

If I Survive You (2022)

Novel by Jonathan Escoffery

BEYOND RACE

According to the 2020 U.S. census, the nation's diversity rate hovers at 61.1 percent. Florida's is 64.1 percent and rising all the time. An impressively large part of that statistic is due to a little neighborhood called Loch Lomond in Pompano Beach, thirty-six miles north of Miami. The mix of Asian, Pacific Islander, Native, Latin American and other minority groups there puts Pompano at an impressive twenty-nine in the nation's ranking of the one hundred most diverse cities. Of its 3,537 residents (at last count), a mere 44 percent were white.

Still, the hero of *If I Survive you*, one of the *New York Times Book Review*'s 100 Notable Books of 2022, would not have fit in there. It's the 1970s, and his parents, Topper and Sanya, have fled Jamaica for Miami, hoping for a better life for their children. They encounter economic hardship and, in 1992, the category 5 monstrosity that was Hurricane Andrew. More to the point, the couple's American-born, younger son Trelawny finds himself an outcast among outcasts, feeling not only the understandable level of estrangement from his immigrant family, but also a broader disenfranchisement from both the white and non-white kids in his world. He is too dark for the Jamaicans, speaks no Spanish and is ignorant of Black American culture. He is a child without a country or, more to the point, a nation unto himself. Nobody will take him in.

"What are you?" ask the young men he thought were his friends. The question, which translates in teen-speak as "Whose side are you on?" is especially relevant in a state whose governor has cut funding—and authorization—for academic diversity, equity and inclusion programs and has overseen the banning of books with these themes.

The hopeful answer in this timely collection of linked stories is that, ultimately, Trelawny is himself and must discover on his own what exactly that entails, as well as what it means to be not simply an American, but also a man. Tellingly, with Escoffery's first story of the eight, which is told in the second person "you," he asks nothing less from us all.

FUN FACT ABOUT *IF I SURVIVE YOU*

This debut collection was shortlisted for the most prestigious literary award in the United Kingdom: the Booker Prize.

Jaws 3-D (1983)

Film Directed by Joe Alves; Starring Dennis Quaid, Bess Armstrong, Louis Gossett Jr., Dolores Starling and Lea Thompson

REVENGE OF THE SHARKS

Readers of this book will be forgiven for thinking that the sequel *Jaws 3-D* should not be included in this volume. Didn't the original hit 1975 movie *Jaws* take place on Massachusetts's Cape Cod? Well, we're not in New England *or* Kansas anymore, and this certainly isn't *Jaws*.

Based on the Peter Benchley bestseller of the same name, the original *Jaws*, directed by Steven Spielberg and starring Roy Scheider, Robert Shaw and Richard Dreyfuss, raked in nearly $500 million and is one of the all-time great horror films. In contrast, the third installment of the series, *Jaws 3-D*, was widely panned. Still, when we're talking Florida, we've got to mention a movie that stars a great white shark or two, a pair of helpful dolphins named Cindy and Sandy and the marine park they inhabit—plus a few bloodied corpses along the way.

Where to begin? While New Smyrna Beach, south of Daytona, is officially known as the "shark bite capital of the world," in 2023 alone, the Florida Program for Shark Research reported sixteen shark bites suffered by unsuspecting swimmers throughout the state.

In this case, the shark is a measly thirty-five feet in length and invades a SeaWorld theme park along with a much smaller shark pal. It kills a number of people and wreaks predictable havoc before being killed—spoiler alert!—by a grenade that is already in its belly and activated by the park's

Is it safe to go back in the water for *Jaws 3-D*? Not when this guy is around. *Wikimedia Commons*.

chief engineer and, coincidentally, the son of Police Chief Mark Brody of Amity Island fame. Seems like those critters just have it in for that family. The real star of the movie is the 3-D effect, which, sadly, cannot be used (along with those cute special glasses) when watching at home, so the home version is titled simply *Jaws III*.

As for marine parks, they are practically Florida's middle name. SeaWorld Orlando, which opened in 1973, welcomed nearly 4.5 million visitors in 2022. Its sister park, Discovery Cove, lets guests interact with animals, including bottlenose dolphins. Swimming with dolphins is a popular tourist pastime throughout Florida, including at the Miami Seaquarium and Theater of the Sea in Islamorada, in the Keys. The USDA has made allegations against some marine theme park owners for taking less than stellar care of its charges, with at least 120 dolphins and whales dying at a single park in recent years. But the parks still operate, and some, such as Theater of the Sea, do tend to injured wild animals as well.

Does that make it better that the sharks take a little revenge in these movies? You be the judge.

FUN FACT ABOUT *JAWS 3-D*

The film was nominated for five awards, if you can call them that—worst picture, director, supporting actor, screenplay and new star (those two dolphins)—at the fourth Golden Raspberry Awards, or Razzies. More humiliating yet, it didn't even win those.

Karen Sisco (2003-04)

TV Series Based on the Novel *Out of Sight* (1996), by
Elmore Leonard; and the Film *Out of Sight* (1998),
Directed by Steven Soderbergh; Starring Carla Gugino,
Robert Forster and Bill Duke

HERE COME THE FEDS

In the movie *Out of Sight*—which only partly takes place in Florida, so it does not get its own listing—Jennifer Lopez plays U.S. deputy marshal Karen Sisco, who, when we first see her, is parked outside the Glades County Detention Center in Belle Glade. She's got her own agenda, but this is quickly forgotten when she catches sight of several escaping inmates climbing out of a tunnel to freedom. Her quick thinking alerts the guards, and several of the escapees are shot. One of them, however, the suave bank robber Jack Foley, enlists the help of his getaway driver to throw her in her own trunk. Foley stays in there with her while the car takes off.

Karen is so clever, cool and confident—as well as alluring—in that first view of her, spooning in her trunk with an escaped con, that it's easy to see why some people thought she deserved a series of her own. As played by Sarasota native Carla Gugino, the series still has her as a federal marshal based in Miami. Now, she's got a retired Miami cop for a dad who doesn't stay in the background nearly as much as he might. She's also got some interesting dates, including one with a Florida Marlins pitcher, although, all in all, her taste in men is pretty lousy. Sadly, the show lasted for only ten episodes. That's right, after just one season, ABC threw in the towel. Apparently *Sisco* faced pretty stiff competition for viewers with the blockbuster *Law and Order* over on rival network NBC.

The show's theme song was the Isley Brothers' 1969 funk single "It's Your Thing." And while its parade of con men, bank robbers, criminal accountants, murderers and counterfeiters certainly did their own thing, it's a shame that Karen Sisco didn't get to do hers a little longer. Still, it was nice to see a woman calling the shots for a while.

By the way, Sisco didn't entirely disappear. She reappeared as Assistant Director Goodall in the same Miami office in the 2012 episode "Cut Ties" of the series *Justified*. Who plays the role? You guessed it: Carla Gugino.

FUN FACT ABOUT *KAREN SISCO*

The series has a place on TV Guide's 2013 list of TV shows that, according to their critics, were "Canceled Too Soon." Also, Elmore Leonard wrote a few short stories about Karen, at least one of which made it into the series. The pilot episode "Blown Away" came from a story of his called "Karen Makes Out."

Key Largo (1948)

Film Directed by John Huston; Based on a 1939 play by
Maxwell Anderson; Starring Humphrey Bogart,
E.G. Robinson and Lauren Bacall

THE MIDDLE OF NOWHERE

When dramatist Maxwell Anderson penned his play about the redemptive
deeds of a Spanish Civil War deserter, its Key Largo setting must have felt
like the absolute end of the Earth, like a place beyond the law. In fact, at
the time, the tiny island (*key* comes from the Spanish word *cayo*, for "islet")
essentially was. It wasn't until after the 1948 film noir became a hit that
many of the island's inhabitants even had an official Key Largo address. In
other words, if Bogey and Bacall's *Key Largo* didn't literally put Key Largo on
the map, it certainly put it on the envelope.

A-list director Huston was not initially pleased. After getting a good look
at the script his producer had pushed on him, he was furious that he had
bought a pig in a poke. Ultimately, the screenwriters changed the period and
many of the details of the original story, but it retained the general crisis: a
cynical antihero becomes a hero despite himself by saving some good people
from death. If you think it sounds a lot like the Bogart classic *Casablanca*, it's
not just you. In this case, the good people in question are the widow and
father of the antihero's army buddy, a true hero of World War II. There is
also a good-sized hurricane, which, to be fair, did not appear in the movie
set in Morocco.

Today, the real thirty-three-mile-long Key Largo, farthest north of the
Florida Keys, is home to about twelve thousand people and has dubbed
itself the "Diving Capital of the World." A mere ninety minutes south of

Bogey and Bacall were one of the greatest onscreen and off-screen couples due to scenes like this in *Key Largo*. *Allstar Picture Library Limited/Alamy Stock Photo.*

bustling Miami, it offers a host of land and sea attractions, from a sprawling state park to cruises on the actual steamboat from yet another Bogart classic, *The African Queen*.

So, why is this movie—yet another that, apart from a few establishing shots, was filmed nowhere near Florida—so important to understanding the state? Because without it, Key Largo might well be just another little island among 1,700.

FUN FACTS ABOUT *KEY LARGO*

Oscar nominee Andy Garcia cowrote and starred in a 2019 theatrical adaptation of the movie in Los Angeles. Also, director John Huston wanted actress Claire Trevor's character, an alcoholic former nightclub entertainer, to appear seriously scared to death when she performed a song a cappella in the movie. He got his way by insisting the non-singing Trevor film it without rehearsing. For her performance, the rightly furious Trevor received an Academy Award for Best Supporting Actress.

A Land Remembered (1984)

Novel by Patrick D. Smith

THE GOOD OLD BAD OLD DAYS

It's Florida's answer to *Gone with the Wind*, minus, for better or for worse, Scarlett O'Hara. *A Land Remembered* is the epic tale of poor Georgia Crackers—not, incidentally, a derogatory term—who arrive in Central Florida a few years before the Civil War and make good and then bad over the next century or so. Smith had already displayed his prodigious knowledge of poverty and the Seminole Tribe, both of which figure in this book, in his earlier historical novels. But it was *Land* that became an international bestseller—and for good reason. For one thing, its chief protagonist, as we will see again and again, was its unforgettable setting.

Like Smith's fictional settlers Tobias MacIvey; his wife, Emma; and his one-year-old son, Zechariah, the author was not a Florida native. Born in a tiny town in Mississippi, he moved to Florida in 1966 at the age of thirty-nine. Yet his ability to capture the spirit of the wilderness, when Florida was one of America's last frontiers—"eaten alive," as he put it in an interview, "with mosquitoes, snakes, alligators, bears, panthers, wolves, swamps, the heat"— rivaled that of another famous non-native, *The Yearling* author, Marjorie Kinnan Rawlings. As Smith once described (with high understatement), "It was some kind of tough."

Land stands out—and has long been assigned in Florida high schools, while younger students read an abridged version—in large part due to the ways in which the descendants of Tobias, who himself had a great love and respect for the pristine environment, came to exploit it for personal gain.

One character, reflecting on how there was a time when people, like animals, took from nature only what they needed, envisions a day when humankind will destroy the Earth. In fact, the later passages of the book can be difficult to get through for lovers of the state, especially when they realize that the McIveys' land was within spitting distance of present-day Disney World. These parts can sometimes read like a how-to manual on pillaging nature.

Smith well knew that the state that supplied the Confederate army with beef from cattle left over after the Spanish occupation was long gone by the time he wrote this book. He knew that many of those who worked to preserve the place were the offspring of Georgia refugees who moved south after their own land was decimated by the Civil War. He knew that values and attitudes had to change in a world with a foundation of concrete rather than humus soil. But he also liked to think that maybe, just maybe, some of the developers who told him they loved the book may have been influenced by it to preserve what is left of the natural landscape.

He has noted that one of them even named a subdivision "*A Land Remembered*."

FUN FACT ABOUT *A LAND REMEMBERED*

Despite its fame in Florida, the book was almost banned from the Indian River Country School District in 2003 for racially offensive language. Also, Smith's research alone took two years to complete.

Live by Night (2012)

Novel by Dennis Lehane

Live by Night (2016)

Film Directed by Ben Affleck; Starring Ben Affleck, Elle Fanning, Zoe Saldana, Sienna Miller, Chris Messina, Chris Cooper and Brendan Gleeson

TO LIVE AND DIE IN TAMPA

To be honest, the first twenty minutes of the movie *Live by Night* take place nowhere near Florida. We see gorgeous sepia stills of a bygone era of World War I soldiers and the politicians, graves and gunmen who followed them into the 1920s and Prohibition. Our hero Joe Coughlin informs us in a voiceover that he promised himself that if he survived the horrendous war as a soldier, he would return to the States as an outlaw, never again to follow another man's rules. At first a small-time crook, he becomes enmeshed, with the help of the absolutely wrong mistress, in a furious feud with an Irish godfather. After the woman's apparent death and three years in prison, he vows revenge, taking a job for the archenemy of his nemesis, an Italian mobster who sends Coughlin to his people in Tampa.

So, we arrive, with plenty of movie (and book) still to go, in Ybor City, a neighborhood northeast of downtown Tampa known for its openness to immigrants and the cigars many of them made. We are introduced to the place's crowded, unpaved streets and the network of tunnels beneath them. We see workers in bustling factories and hear the Cuban music in fancy clubs. And we get a bloody taste of the machinations of the kind of

Cigar makers employed readers for news and education in Ybor City, the setting for *Live by Night*. *Wikimedia Commons*.

organized crime that really existed there in the 1920s, when the Ybor mob ran, among other things, over three hundred *bolita* houses, where local Latin American, Italian and Black men lost their hard-earned cash in a lottery-type gambling game.

This is not the only movie to have been shot in Ybor City; there are at least eight others. And it's not hard to see why. The fascinating location reminds us that, yes, there are historic places in the state besides St. Augustine that date all the way back to 1886 and further, and many of them are extremely colorful. In other words, people may come for Disney World, but they should stay for the real world.

FUN FACTS ABOUT *LIVE BY NIGHT*

Leonardo DeCaprio was intended for the lead role, but he decided to produce instead, leaving the part to Affleck. Also, the original cut of the movie ran nearly three hours; it was eventually released with a run time of a little over two hours.

Magic City (2012-13)

TV Series Created by Mitch Glazer; Starring
Jeffrey Dean Morgan, Olga Kurylenko, Steven Strait,
Jessica Marais, Christian Cooke and Danny Huston

MOBSTER METROPOLIS

The year 1959 is dawning, and the rebel Fidel Castro has just recently wrested Cuba from the claws of the dictator Fulgencio Batista y Zalvídar. Meanwhile, 225 miles away in Miami, the owner of the fictitious Miramar Playa, the city's most luxurious hotel, is, against his better judgment, doing business with the vicious mobster Ben "The Butcher" Diamond in order to keep the struggling business afloat.

In the period immediately following the Cuban Revolution, Havana and Miami were possibly never closer, geographically or culturally, with the flow of drugs, evildoers and money turned on full blast for anyone who had a certain combination of luck, money, bravery, foolhardiness, connections and, in some cases, government jobs. In *Magic City*, the glamour and grisliness of the period are in close proximity to the adultery, blackmail, bribery and CIA wiretaps that accompany any lively series about the intermingling of politics and a certain kind of business.

An interesting idea, exquisite set design and costumes, intelligent direction, appearances by Alex Rocco and James Caan (*The Godfather*), as well as Sherilyn Fenn and Esai Morales, along with the regular cast, gave the series the look and feel of the period that creator and writer Glazer was after. Somehow, however, despite critical acclaim, the series never really found itself a large enough audience, and even a planned 2014 movie adaptation with Hollywood heavyweights Bruce Willis and Bill Murray didn't materialize. The reasons for this are unclear. The cool, cynical view of the underbelly of that period, which is often a subject for nostalgia, may have been too much for modern-day audiences, who were already in the grips of *Mad Men*, AMC's New York–based mega-hit that ran from 2007 to 2015. What's more, unlike, say, the mobster-themed *Sopranos*, which had wrapped five years earlier, *Magic City* is by no means a comedy, black or otherwise.

It's a shame, really, because Miami Beach in that period was an extraordinary world unto itself. Come to think of it, you might say it still is.

FUN FACT ABOUT *MAGIC CITY*

The series drew from the personal experience of creator Mitch Glazer, as well as that of his father, who worked in the world of posh Miami Beach hotels in days gone by.

Magic Mike (2012)

Film Directed by Steven Soderbergh; Starring Channing Tatum, Joe Manganiello, Matt Bomer, Alex Pettyfer and Matthew McConaughey

HOT PANTS

According to at least one online source, Florida has the most strip clubs of any state in the United States—243—and the second all-around best clubs, some of which are in Tampa. An eighteen-year-old Channing Tatum's experience dancing in one of those Tampa clubs under the name Chan Crawford led to the development of not one, not two but *three* movies about his character Mike Lane, who, in this first outing, shows a young man the ropes at the Xquisite Strip Club, where he has worked for six years and become the star dancer.

Although—spoiler alert!—Mike decides to leaves the stripping life behind at the end of the first movie, the two sequels, *Magic Mike XXL* and *Magic Mike's Last Dance* (some of which take place in Florida but are also set in South Carolina and London), demonstrate that he returns for a lack of better options. And this fact, apart from the luscious loins of young men and the lascivious looks of their audiences, is the point of these movies. Tatum, who grew up in rural Mississippi and Tampa, got his start in Orlando as a dancer on a music video. His boy-next-door good looks led to modeling jobs, commercials and, eventually, films. But with diagnoses of dyslexia and ADD, he might have gone in a very different direction had he had a different face or body. That is to say, stripping, considered a shameful profession by large swaths of society, is also an important source of income for many working-class people. It's also, if this movie is any indication, hard work.

Magic Mike was partly based on Channing Tatum's own experiences. *AJ Pics/Alamy Stock Photo.*

Magic Mike, shot partly in West Florida locations like Tampa, Ybor City, Tarpon Springs, Dunedin and St. Petersburg, isn't exactly the most profound look at the plight of blue collar workers in America. But it probably is the sexiest, and the first film was a hit with critics and made a killing at the box office. And that, says Tatum, who coproduced the sequels, is just fine with him.

FUN FACT ABOUT *MAGIC MIKE*

Matthew McConaughey did not initially have a dance number in the script; it was added at his request. Also, the movies spawned a short-lived HBO reality competition show and a musical adaptation in London.

Miami (1991)

Novel by Pat Booth

THIS IS NOT YOUR FATHER'S MIAMI BEACH

There was a time not so long ago when the idea of pouting supermodels slipping in and out of limousines around South Miami Beach would have been laughable. Long before it was nicknamed SoBe, the neighborhood east of Miami proper, located south of Dade Boulevard, between Biscayne Bay and the Atlantic, was home to poor, geriatric men and women with walkers finishing out their meager lives among some of the few apartment houses in Florida that welcomed Jews after the mid-1920s, as well as drug addicts and a fair number of equally hapless Cubans. The entertainer Jackie Gleason reigned supreme for a while, but since the mid-1980s, thanks in large part to those shimmering location shots of *Miami Vice*, the area and its reputation began to explode. By the end of that decade, the fashion industry had established a firm heel print in the area, with world-famous photographers posing beautiful people in front of the pastel-colored, refurbished Art Deco façades. In those heady days, the name Gianni Versace, as well as Madonna, was everywhere. Today, the neighborhood is a little tamer, perhaps, but it's even richer, in more ways than one. It's home to an exotic mix of languages, gender identifications, night life and, perhaps most importantly, currencies.

Booth's modern-day bodice ripper is a paean to the rich, famous and wannabes in South Beach in the form of its main characters: the world's current top model Lisa Rodriguez and former supermodel and mogul-in-the-making Christa Kenwood. These two are juxtaposed with Christa's new client and soon-to-be enemy, Palm Beach billionaire Mary Whitney, whom we encounter both in her home city and farther south. While Kenwood grew up in tony Palm Beach and has come to know the rules and the players of both worlds, Whitney is a diehard blue blood. The tug-of-war among the women, as well as the tumultuous affairs between Kenwood and a serious Key West novelist and between Rodriguez and a quickly lapsed Christian Adonis demonstrate the perspective of former model Booth on new money versus old, commerce versus art, women versus men and, ultimately, in the form of a monstrous modeling agency maestro, bad versus worse.

Nobody comes out of this square dance with clean hands, but that's not the point of the novel or of Booth's earlier tome *Palm Beach* and other bestsellers. As Freud might have put it, Palm Beach is South Florida's ego; Miami is its id. All the steamy sex scenes in the world—and most of them are probably in these pages—do not belie Booth's philosophy: if you are beautiful enough, strong enough, talented enough and lucky enough, you can have it all. And it's all available for the taking in the new, larger-than-life Miami.

FUN FACT ABOUT *MIAMI*

The clubs Warsaw and Mezzanotte mentioned in the novel are real locations, and eagle-eyed readers will spot a number of actual personalities by the names of Kennedy, Hutton and Trump.

Miami Blues (1984)

Novel by Charles Willeford

Miami Blues (1990)

Film Directed by George Armitage; Starring Alec Baldwin, Fred Ward and Jennifer Jason Leigh

THE BAD OLD DAYS

Forty years is a lot of calendar pages in the life of a major American city. When Charles Willeford penned his ode to cops and robbers in Miami and Miami Beach, there was a ban on new construction on South Beach, and the place was filled with long-past-their-prime hotels and apartment buildings populated by poor, aging Jews. But times have changed. Today, South Beach is code for hip, loud, model-gorgeous and "can't get a table." The old Art Deco buildings have been restored to their former glory and then some. For the last couple of decades, the area has even had a fad diet named after it.

The neo-noir modern classic novel *Miami Blues* is first narrated from the point of view of recent California transplant and ex-felon Frederick J. Frenger Jr., also known as Junior, also known as the name printed on whatever license and credit card he's happened to rip off most recently. The book then bounces back and forth between Junior's life of crime without punishment and the meager existence of a sad sack Miami cop, Sergeant Hoke Moseley, whom Junior viciously assaults. We know from the beginning that, against all odds, Moseley will get his man, but we don't see, as in any good thriller, any possible source of his salvation. Moseley is, albeit only in his forties, not in the best of shape, while Junior is trouble with a capital T-R-O-U-B-L-E.

Downtown Miami is the setting for *Miami Blues*. *Wikimedia Commons.*

What we do see, although indirectly, is the juxtaposition of the little town of Okeechobee, 130 miles north of Miami, and the home of Junior's newly minted "platonic wife," Miami-Dade College student-cum-hooker Susie Waggoner, and her freshly dead brother Martin, who wanted nothing more than to own a Burger King franchise and to have his ashes, when the time came, scattered over the nearby lake. The largest freshwater lake in the state, Lake Okeechobee, got its name from the Hitchiti words for "big water." (There's a Seminole story in which the lake was created from a young boy who turned into a snake.) At over 700 square miles wide, it provides drinking water for millions of South Florida residents and is also said to provide the best bass fishing on the planet. When the book was written, marine biologists had just started worrying about the impact of phosphorous from the sugar industry on the lake, which subsequently grew into a major environmental catastrophe.

True, we don't actually get a gander at the lake in this story, although we hear about it several times. And yes, criminals like Junior have been a fixture in this part of the state for well over a century—and still are. Still, *Miami Blues* harkens back to a time when life was simpler. When a bad guy *and* a pissed-off cop would take the trouble to steal a policeman's set of false teeth. When the 125,000 Cuban "Marielitos" had come to the city recently enough to be recognized as such. When many more parts of South Florida actually *were* a lot calmer than Miami. And when out-of-staters criticized Florida drivers and Florida humidity.

On second thought, maybe the city isn't that different after all.

FUN FACT ABOUT *MIAMI BLUES*

When an audience in New Jersey previewed the movie before it was released, they were furious that Fred Ward's good-guy cop killed Alec Baldwin's bad-guy character.

Miami Noir (2006)

Anthology Edited by Les Standiford

HOT, HUMID AND HORRIFIC

The atmosphere is the main character in this grisly anthology of murder and mayhem in Miami, which is entirely appropriate, when you think about it. The word *noir*, which means "black" in French, refers to a genre, originally in film, that not only examines the darkness in the hearts of its characters but is also shot, if not always literally in black and white, with a fair amount of shadow. Characters tend to talk like Bogart in *The Maltese Falcon*, an early icon of the genre. Think world-weary antiheroes facing hardened criminals with a soupçon of existential dread.

That this all plays out in Miami is hardly a coincidence. For one thing, it is one entry in a series of noir anthologies put out by the same publisher that feature major metropolises known for major bad behavior. More than that, as a character notes in Lynne Barrett's "The Noir Boudoir," Miami is awash in immigrant murderers: drug lords who have restyled themselves as developers, dictators who now own steakhouses and death squad killers who earn a living, if not always an honest one, as mechanics. In this scenario, the sun-glazed streets are in fact awash in blood, but it's usually just beneath the surface.

Unless it's not. As backdrop to murder, we see all the usual suspects here. A reference to Stiltsville, the 1930s landmark on Key Biscayne that was once a twenty-seven-residence community of elevated shacks in the middle of Biscayne Bay. An appearance by Tobacco Road, a popular dive bar that opened in 1912 and served time as a speakeasy and a music venue before closing its doors in 2014. A nod to dominoes-playing Cuban emigres in José Marti Park, who left the island nation when Castro came to power. A hungry alligator in a pool. An electric saw, originally purchased to clean up after Hurricane Andrew, now repurposed for easy body disposal. A Santería ritual and the memory of the once-stately and now-defunct Hialeah Racetrack. An ode to the South River. And, of course, South Beach and the Art Deco Delano Hotel on Collins Avenue.

The stories, which all feature a particular neighborhood or region of the Miami Metropolitan area, be it Coconut Grove, Homestead, Sunny Isles or the Upper Eastside, are nearly all heavy in their descriptions and geographical references, making them particularly engaging for those in the know. And the collection's authors know of what they speak. A good number of them are graduates or faculty of Florida International University's MFA creative writing program, including editor Les Standiford, the founding director, who is no stranger to Miami crime fiction in his own successful writing career.

Miami Purity (1995)

Novel by Vicki Hendricks

HOLD THE STARCH

Her name is Sherish (Sherri) Parlay, and she is a former exotic dancer with a penchant for peppermint schnapps and murder. He is Payne Mahoney, of the "Jagger lips." Together, they turn up the steam in a dry-cleaning establishment in North Miami owned by Payne's mother and ironically known as Miami Purity. Hendricks's neo-noir debut, based on James M. Cain's 1934 classic *The Postman Always Rings Twice*, depicts a certain strata of society that exists in most every town across America. These are people who live on the edges, from paycheck to paycheck and, at least when sober, wouldn't dream of participating in Take Your Daughter to Work Day.

In this version, Ms. Parlay is in her mid-thirties, ready to quit boozing and dancing after disposing of a husband who, to be fair, was plenty abusive. And she tries. Lord knows she tries. The problem is that she can't stop herself from jumping up on a bar table on her lunch break and reverting to her previous profession, free of charge. Or from coming up with a new and creative way to dispose of her, shall we say, dirty laundry.

So, yes, there are Sherri Parlays everywhere. Exotic dancing, however, has taken hold of South Florida in a big way. Maybe it's the fact that it's already so warm outside, the women don't have as many clothes to take off in the first place. With names like the Booby Trap and TheXXXZone, adult entertainment venues are alive and well here, and there is something for pretty much every taste. It's big business, too, even sometimes for the entertainers themselves. But many of them lose a little of their soul with every twerk.

Which is where Sherri comes in. At minimum wage in the pedestrian world of dry cleaning, she knows she will not make what she made in tips in her old life. But when she takes one look at the young man behind the counter, she sees, like so many who come to Florida, a way to clean the slate and start fresh—get it?—to reinvent herself. The problem is, although we may leave the snow of Cleveland or wherever far behind, we always take ourselves with us. It's a hard-won lesson for many Florida transplants. And it gets repeated every day of every year.

FUN FACT ABOUT *MIAMI PURITY*

Hendricks began the novel as a master of fine arts degree course assignment.

Miami Vice (1984–89)

TV Series Created by Anthony Yerkovich; Starring
Don Johnson and Philip Michael Thomas,
Saundra Santiago, Michael Talbott,
Edward James Olmos and Olivia Brown

THE CITY IS OURS

The word on *Miami Vice* is that in one of those interesting examples of life imitating art, the world-famous TV show supposedly made Miami what it is today. To be sure, the award-winning series, which aired on NBC, ushered in a new level of cool, with celebrity culture, pricey-perfect-pastel-colored buildings on South Beach and an emphasis on popular music, style and fashion hitherto unknown in the Magic City. And did I mention crime?

In fact, when it comes to crime, art very much imitated life. Antisocial behavior was a popular Miami activity long before *Vice* creator Yerkovich called the city "a sort of Barbary Coast of free enterprise gone berserk." In the late 1920s, it was the winter home of legendary Chicago mobster Al Capone, who died in his Palm Island mansion in 1947. Ma Barker spent some time there as well, and not-too-distant neighbors engaged in running speakeasies, rumrunning, piracy and other illicit activity. Cuba strongman Fidel Castro's 1980 export of nearly 125,000 of his people—known as the Mariel Boatlift—helped him empty the streets and prisons of not only political protestors but also bona fide criminals, expanding the entrenched Cuban and Central American communities in Miami, some of whom had easy access to cocaine and other illegal substances.

Enter Sonny Crockett and former New Yorker Ricardo "Rico" Tubbs, who tooled around in designer suits and a white Ferrari Testarossa. How,

Miami Vice stars Don Johnson and Philip Michael Thomas helped change the city forever. *AJ Pics/Alamy Stock Photo.*

you may ask, could cops afford the duds and wheels unless they were on the take? According to the show, it was all thanks to asset forfeiture statutes, which allowed their department to hold onto the ill-gotten gains of drug lords in pursuit of more evildoers. In fact, it was those statutes that gave Yerkovich the idea for the series in the first place. Great-looking cops, great-looking location, fabulous lifestyle! A perfect storm of television show qualities.

Did someone mention celebrity culture? The show was so hip that it not only inspired well-known musicians, such as Miles Davis, Glenn Frey, Isaac Hayes, Ted Nugent, Leonard Cohen, Phil Collins, Little Richard, Gene Simmons and Frank Zappa to take up a life of fictional crime, but it also made use of some of their music. Producers paid as much as $10,000 for the of-the-moment popular music for the show's montages. It also brought in future A-list actors, like Helena Bonham Carter, Bruce Willis, Julia Roberts, Benicio del Toro, Viggo Mortensen, Chris Rock and—in a speaking role— the famously mute Teller of the magic act Penn and Teller.

No doubt about it: *Miami Vice* changed television. It also helped change Miami.

FUN FACTS ABOUT *MIAMI VICE*

Actors originally considered for the role of Sonny Crockett included Nick Nolte, Mickey Rourke, Larry Wilcox of *CHiPs* and Jeff Bridges. Also, Mark Harmon was ready to replace Johnson when the star had trouble renegotiating his contract after season two, but he and the network finally agreed to new terms. What's more, sales of the RayBan Wayfarer style skyrocketed after a pair of the sunglasses was added to Crockett's wardrobe.

Monster (2003)

Film Directed by Patty Jenkins; Starring Charlize Theron, Christina Ricci, Bruce Dern and Lee Tergesen

THE ROAD TO DEATH ROW

The first recorded female serial killer in the United States, Aileen Carol Wuornos, never got to see the dramatized story of her crime spree. She was executed by lethal injection in 2002. Although she was sentenced to death for only six murders, Wuornos, who already had a criminal record for theft and armed robbery, purportedly killed seven of her male clients off Florida highways in northern and central Florida in the space of a year.

Originally sent to the now-defunct Broward Correctional Institution near Pembroke Pines, Wuornos sat for over a decade on death row at Florida State (Raiford) Prison in Bradford County. During this time, she unsuccessfully appealed to the U.S. Supreme Court for clemency. Although the court ruled capital punishment unconstitutional in 1972, thereby causing Florida to commute the sentences of ninety-six inmates to life imprisonment, the court overturned its ruling in 1976, and executions resumed in the state three years later. Since 1976, just over one hundred executions have taken place at the prison, with as many as eight occurring in both 1984 and 2014. Since 2000, the state legislature has allowed lethal injection as an alternative to the electric chair.

Wuornos's real-life girlfriend, Tyria Moore, was called Selby Wall in the film, and her first victim, Richard Mallory, was renamed Vincent Corey. Otherwise, most of the details are true. Wuornos was born in Michigan and did attempt to kill herself numerous times. In addition, she did meet her girlfriend at a gay bar in Daytona Beach, and she was arrested at a biker bar. What's more, Moore did eventually cooperate with the police, which led to Wuornos's conviction and execution.

Apart from the execution, perhaps the most important detail of both the film and the true story is the traumatic sexual abuse that Wuornos suffered as a child, including a rape that led her to a home for unwed mothers at the age of fourteen. Mitigating circumstances were clearly not considered important enough to commute the killer's sentence to life imprisonment—but that's possibly because she was a sex worker. And although Wuornos fiercely denied it, experts concluded that she also suffered from mental illness, due to either her family history (her father, Leo Dale Pittman, was in and out of mental hospitals and served time for statutory rape prior to his apparent death by suicide) or the harm she suffered early in her development.

Terrible story. Memorable movie.

FUN FACTS ABOUT *MONSTER*

Noted film critic Roger Ebert considered Charlize Theron's performance— she was the first South African to win an Oscar for Best Actress—"one of the great performances in the history of cinema." Also, the ultra-glamorous Theron reportedly gained thirty pounds for the role.

Moon Over Miami (1941)

Film Directed by Walter Lang, from the Movie *Three Blind Mice* (1938), Based on the Play by Stephen Powys; Starring Betty Grable, Don Ameche, Robert Cummings, Carole Landis, Jack Haley and Charlotte Greenwood

HUSBAND SHOPPING

In the movie *Three Blind Mice*, produced before World War II, three sisters from Kansas use their disappointingly small inheritances to score husbands in California. In the version called *Moon Over Miami* that came out three years later, they lose a sister, gain an aunt, hail from Texas and set off for Miami. They also sing their hearts out in their attempt to score Grable—she of the million-dollar legs—a millionaire husband. Hijinks ensue, and by the end of the film, all three women are getting hitched.

So, why the decision to relocate the setting to Miami? For one thing, the title song, written by Joe Burke and Edgar Leslie in 1935 and recorded over the years by the likes of Patti Page, Bill Haley and the Comets, Ray Charles, the Platters and Percy Faith, just wouldn't have had the same appeal if it had been titled "Moon Over California." ("Constellation Over California"?)

For another, up-and-coming Miami was already poised to play an important role during World War II. From early 1942 to 1945, Miami Beach hotels housed a U.S. Army Air Corps training base, while the Biltmore Hotel was used as a hospital for wounded soldiers returning from the front. What's more, radar was mostly developed at the army airfield just up the road in Boca Raton, at the present site of the Florida Atlantic University campus. True, the United States hadn't entered the war before the Japanese attacked Pearl Harbor on December 7, 1941, after which the U.S. Army Air Corps took command of Miami Beach, but there were many who had anticipated it soon after Hitler's troops invaded Poland in 1939, so preparations were in the making.

Speaking of history, the moviemakers couldn't have known it at the time, but the real Miami Beach location of the Flamingo Hotel setting is now a thing of the past. It was torn down in the 1950s to pave the way for the Morton Towers development, now the Flamingo South Beach.

FUN FACTS ABOUT *MOON OVER MIAMI*

The nationwide Denny's diner chain serves a popular omelette dish called Moon Over My Hammy, which is a ham and scrambled egg sandwich with American and Swiss cheese on two nice slabs of grilled bread, with hash browns on the side. Also, in 1935, two Jewish New York Giants baseball players, Phil Weintraub and Harry Danning, were denied entry to the Flamingo hotel due to its being "restricted." In other words, it was open to gentiles only. The management eventually backed down from their demand to send the two players to another hotel, however, when the ball team informed them that it would move all the players, not just the two Jewish ones, if they didn't get room keys.

Moonlight (2016)

Film Directed by Barry Jenkins; Starring
Travante Rhodes, Mahershala Ali, Naomie Harris,
Ashton Sanders, Jharrel Jerome, Janelle Monáe
and André Holland

LOVE IN LIBERTY CITY

It was the film that "broke" the Oscars. When *Moonlight* was finally—after an on-air ballot mix-up—awarded the Academy Award for Best Picture at the awards show, it was a pivotal moment, not just for all those associated with the film but also for the people the film was about. People who were poor, Black, addicted to drugs and/or gay in Miami's Liberty City neighborhood and beyond finally had an acclaimed movie that spoke to and for them. How acclaimed? The first major movie to focus on LGBTQ themes in the Black community was nominated for eight Oscars and took home three, along with plenty of other honors.

The Liberty City neighborhood of Miami has one of the largest concentrations of Black residents in South Florida. Developed during the 1930s, the housing project, once known as Model City, was intended to be a corrective to the slums of nearby Overtown. During a time of extreme segregation, it served as a thriving middle-class neighborhood. By the 1960s, however, due to highway construction and integration, vulnerable residents from Overtown had moved into the area, and it became a magnet for poverty and crime. *Miami Vice* helped bring the problems of the area to national attention. More recently, climate change is beginning to have a positive effect on property values in the neighborhood, as Liberty City's higher elevation, along with that of Little Haiti, is making it attractive to outside investors.

Moonlight was an Oscar upset for best picture in more ways than one. *FlixPix/Alamy Stock Photo.*

The movie focuses on Liberty City at the height of the crack epidemic. Unfolding in three parts as the main character evolves from childhood as Little, to youth as Chiron and then adulthood as Black, it chronicles the pain and progress of a shy child of a crack addict mother, who is bullied for being different and must figure out how to make a life for himself with the help of a local drug dealer and his girlfriend.

Tarell Alvin McCraney, who wrote and lived *In Moonlight Black Boys Look Blue*—an unpublished manuscript on which the movie is based—says that his hometown of Liberty City is still beautiful. Many people might be surprised to hear that, but then many people would be surprised at a plot in which a drug dealer makes a positive difference in a lonely boy's life. *Moonlight* demonstrates that even amid addiction, poverty and cruelty, there is kindness and beauty. That realization is a kind of liberty in its own right.

Naked Came the Manatee (1996)

Novel by Carl Hiaasen, Elmore Leonard, Dave Barry,
James W. Hall, Edna Buchanan, Les Standiford, Paul Levine,
Brian Antoni, Tananarive Due, John Dufresne,
Vicki Hendricks, Carolina Hospital and Evelyn Mayerson

GROUP PROJECT

In 1969, New York's *Newsday* columnist Mike McGrady commissioned two dozen colleagues to contribute a chapter each to a potpourri of a salacious novel under a single pseudonym, thereby proving that American literature was, if not in the toilet, then snugly situated in the bedroom. The result of the trick was a lurid, poorly written bestseller called *Naked Came the Stranger*. This is not that book.

For one thing, a mere thirteen writers contributed to *Manatee* under their own names. For another, none of their extremely well-written prose was dumbed down by the editors, as was the case with *Stranger*. For better or for worse, nudity, apart from a 102-year-old woman who swims with a manatee, does not abound. And instead of New York writers working with a Long Island, New York, setting, the Florida-authored *Manatee* takes place in, you guessed it, Miami, with several of the contributors connected in one way or another to the MFA program at Florida International University. (Full disclosure: so was the author of this book.)

For the most part, the novel, nutty as it is, works. With one or two exceptions, it reads as though it was written by a single author rather than through a game of literary telephone serialized in the *Tropic* magazine supplement of the *Miami Herald*. The madcap plot features the combined efforts of the characters from the better-known authors' individual crime series, who never found themselves inhabiting the same book before—or since.

Looking for the point of a book like this is like inquiring about the price of a sixteen-bedroom mansion on Biscayne Bay. If you've got to ask, in other words, fugettaboutit. But as a pleasurable introduction to some of the fictional and actual stars of Miami noir and a diverting romp with environmental undertones through some beautiful landscape, *Manatee* delivers. It proves that when it comes to the state of crime fiction in the state of Florida, all is well.

Just don't expect many nude marine mammals.

The Nickel Boys (2019)

Novel by Colson Whitehead

Nickel Boys (2024)

Film Directed by RaMell Ross; Starring Aunjanue Ellis-Taylor, Ethan Herisse, Fred Hechinger, Hamish Linklater and Daveed Diggs

REFORMING THE REFORMERS

It should come as no surprise that *The Nickel Boys* won the 2020 Pulitzer Prize for Fiction, Whitehead's second win after his 2016 novel about slavery, *The Underground Railroad*. Due to its unsparing portrait of reform school abuse in Jim Crow Florida, Whitehead's book touched a nerve at a time when the horrors suffered by children in boarding schools in not only the United States but also Australia and Canada were coming to light for the general public. Whitehead's novel does what only fiction can: it puts us in the heads and behind the eyes of a variety of people who lived the events, in this case, Elwood Curtis, who was sent to the school for a crime he did not commit, and the unforgettable friend he makes there named Turner.

The fictional Nickel Academy is based on the real-life Florida School for Boys, also known as the Arthur G. Dozier School for Boys, which Whitehead says he learned about on Twitter only a few years before he started working on the book. At one time, Dozier was the nation's largest reform school. The State of Florida ran it between 1900 and 2011 in Marianna, a city in the Panhandle near the Georgia border. Although claims of sexual violence, torture—boys were reportedly isolated and hogtied for weeks at a time, and

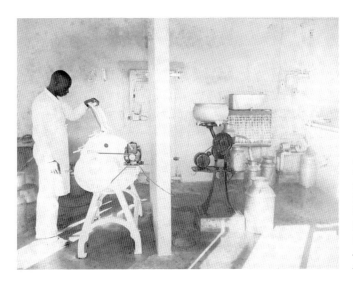

A student works the dairy machine at the infamous Dozier School for Boys, the model for the school in *The Nickel Boys*. *State Archives of Florida*.

a student lost his arm in a washing machine—beatings and murder, all at the hands of school employees, were made for decades and multiple inspections caused administrators to come and go, it was only in 2010 that the Florida Department of Law Enforcement launched a full-scale investigation, which was followed by the U.S. Department of Justice's Civil Rights Division's investigations the following year. Forensic anthropologist Erin Kimmerle at the University of South Florida then began her own research a year after that. She identified more than fifty-five graves on the property and found compelling evidence of close to one hundred deaths that occurred at the school. One of her findings: three times more Black students died at Dozier than white students, which reflected the school's population.

"If there's one place like this, there are many," Whitehead said in an interview. Dozier was part of Florida's history, but at least it's not part of its future.

FUN FACTS ABOUT *THE NICKEL BOYS*

In 2024, the Florida legislature approved $20 million to compensate victims of the school. Also, the movie is director Ross's narrative feature film debut.

Ninety-Two in the Shade (1972)
Novel by Thomas McGuane

A LONG, STRANGE TRIP

It's hot, sure, but what's really smoking in this fever dream of a novel is Tom Skelton's brain. Freshly off good, long highs farther north in Gainesville and Homestead, young Tom hitchhikes back home to Key West, where he reunites with his worried mother; nonsensical father, who has taken to living in a bassinet; and no-nonsense grandfather, a crooked former state senator. Each family member wants to support him in their own eccentric way, which soon comes to mean simply keeping him alive.

But why should he die? The plot involves Skelton's plan to become a flats fishing guide, taking tourists out among the mangroves for permit and bonefish. It's a time-honored Key West occupation, and two men have it more or less sewn up on the island: Faron Carter and known killer Nicholl Dance. However, When Dance plays a prank on Skelton during his first trip out on a borrowed skiff, Skelton turns around and burns up the older man's boat. This leads to the threat that if Skelton ever guides again, he is a dead man. That's what this slim volume is leading up to.

It all sounds perfectly clear. But when we factor in Skelton's grandfather making love on a trampoline, plus his own barking—you read that right—in and out of his digs in a fuselage from a navy reconnaissance plane parked next door to a rundown hotel, in which an alcoholic ex-drill sergeant takes his "army" of drunks through their paces each day at 7:00 a.m., we begin to realize that we are not only in Thomas McGuane territory but also the anything-goes Key West, a republic all its own. This, after all, is the proudly independent Conch Republic, so dubbed in 1982 for its (mostly in jest) initiative to leave the United States. This is the birthplace of the laid-back tropical "Margaritaville" lifestyle, based on the 1977 hit song by Jimmy Buffett, Key West's most famous resident after—or even including—one Ernest Hemingway.

McGuane's hallucinogenic prose is a perfect reflection of a certain kind of life, in which grown men spend so many hours out in the sun on the water in pursuit of adventure and death that they can't help but return to land with their brains a little fried. Add to that another time-honored Key West tradition, partying, and we're not always sure where our segues are in our own stories, not to mention this one.

Apart from his characters' prey, McGuane, a lifelong conservationist, shows us a pristine and magical land populated with plenty of snapper, sharks and sprats, plus a fair number of catbirds, anhingas, cormorants, pelicans and cranes. Most of all, he displays a way of life through a lens loaded with so much Vaseline that we can scarcely see straight—which is just fine. Through the haze, we know that we are in a whole other land. In fact, it's a whole other world.

Nip/Tuck (2003-10; 2003-06, Set in Florida)

TV Series Created by Ryan Murphy; Starring Dylan Walsh, Julian McMahon, John Hensley and Joely Richardson

THE DOCTOR IS IN—TROUBLE

So what if the fictional McNamara/Troy plastic surgery center moved from Miami to Los Angeles mid-series? *Nip/Tuck*, the often-grisly, blackly humorous drama that follows the woes, worries and woman trouble of best friends and partners Sean McNamara and Christian Troy and their various employees, lovers and patients, is the quintessential South Florida show. There may be more plastic surgeons in California, but on a per capita basis, Florida beats it by a well-shaped nose. In fact, in a 2016 report, already several years after the show went off the air, it was reported that Miami actually had the highest number of plastic surgeons of any city, and the ratio of these docs to residents was nearly four for every one hundred thousand. Now *that's* a lot of potential butt lifts and tummy tucks.

And it makes sense. For one thing, South Florida is a good lifestyle choice for the professionals. While Los Angeles is home to plenty of aging (and ageless) movie stars, Miami has a comparatively less hectic lifestyle, just right for your talented MD who wants to get away from it all without getting away from all of it. Culture also plays a role. The large, wealthy Latin American population in the city and in nations in close proximity is extremely looks-conscious: Venezuela, for instance, has had the most beauty contest wins of any nation, with seven Miss Universes alone. And let's not forget the population of models and other beautiful people in South Beach, where the

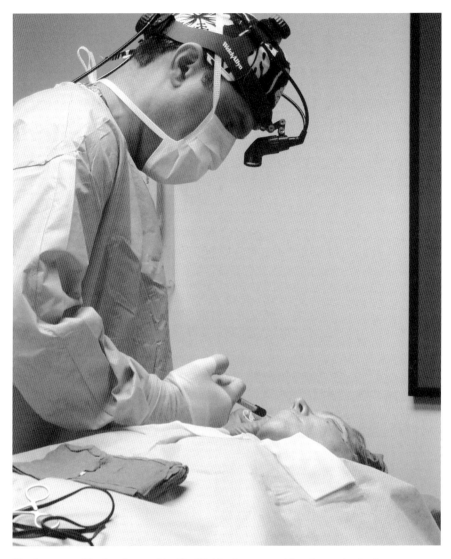

Plastic surgery like that featured in *Nip/Tuck* is almost considered non-elective in some Florida circles. *Wikimedia Commons.*

series was first set, who make the rest of us, particularly those who can afford it, eager to raise our game.

The controversial series features topics like serial murder, adultery, rape and porn stardom, but its heart, in more ways than one, are the patients, for which each episode is named. Their plights range from sixteen-year-olds who "fix" less-than-perfect noses to a morbidly obese woman literally grafted onto her couch and a billionaire who wants his testicles enlarged (to the size of kiwis, in case you were wondering). One of the things that caused the show to raise eyebrows was the often cavalier approach to cosmetic enhancement. Another was the graphic and often gross depiction of the blood-and-guts work of surgeons. Watch a leaky silicone implant extraction, and it may cure you of vanity forever. On the other hand, you may be into that sort of thing. In its debut season, *Nip/Tuck* was the highest rated new series ever shown on American basic cable.

Speaking of beautiful people, viewers are treated to a variety of guest stars, some of whom, like Catherine Deneuve, Jacqueline Bisset, Sharon Gless, Larry Hagman and Vanessa Redgrave, were, fittingly, a few years past their prime and most likely had themselves spent some time under a knife or two. Art imitating life imitating art imitating life? Hmmm. Sounds like Miami.

FUN FACTS ABOUT *NIP/TUCK*

Mentiras Perfectas was a Spanish-language adaptation of the show, produced in Colombia in 2013. The title means "Perfect Lies." Also, the show inspired a reality show called *Dr. 90210*. If the zip code sounds familiar, it was the title of another tony Los Angeles–based series about beautiful people gone bad.

On Becoming a God in Central Florida (2019)

TV Series Created by Robert Funke and Matt Lutsky;
Starring Kirsten Dunst, Théodore Pellerin,
Mel Rodriguez, Beth Ditto and Ted Levine

SMASHING THE PYRAMIDS

In the 1939 movie *Gone with the Wind*, Scarlett O'Hara memorably says, "I'll never go hungry again!" She wasn't in Florida at the time, but when Krystal Stubbs says, "I won't be poor again!" we know that she is channeling that other great Southern belle. Scarlett married up. Krystal, however, is a modern woman. She decided to go up against Founders American Merchandise, handily nicknamed FAM. Based on something like Amway, the multilevel marketing system (or direct selling, or pyramid scheme) is portrayed here as the sort of nonreligious cult that capitalism breeds so well. And Krystal, whose life savings are in the company, has had enough. Enough of the bankrupting upfront costs. Enough of the catechism (known here as the Garbeau System to Getting Rich). Enough of the sham. She is mad as hell, and she is not going to take it anymore.

Let's face it: Florida is awash in fraud. These days, the state is battling, among other schemes, cryptocurrency scams, fake checks, scammers posing as law enforcement officers and even UPS package scams. And let's not forget those emails the elderly receive, supposedly from their grandchildren trapped in a foreign country asking for a couple of thousand dollars to get out. One might think that Florida is a target because of its high percentage of unwitting seniors, or because it's just such a big state, or because of the Wild

West mentality that is an important part of our ethos. This is all true. But Florida also has a long, strong history of fraud. "I've got some swampland in Florida to sell you" is a cliché for a reason. Over the last one hundred years or more, many plots of land have been sold sight unseen to unsuspecting northerners who wanted to get in on the ground floor of the latest frontier. Some of these deals panned out. A lot of them ruined their eager owners.

The series opens in the Orlando area in 1992. Krystal, a former pageant queen and water park employee, is a new mom with a husband who buys into the FAM scheme before—spoiler alert—he dies in a very Florida way. (Think long tail and big jaws.) The "Alligator Widow," as she is soon known, proceeds to take off her braces (in a memorable scene) and do what the system has taught her: visualize, strategize and actualize. Except her trainers thought she would be selling soap, not taking over their company.

It's fun, it's violent, it's over the top to the point of being more than a bit surreal. No, I don't mean Florida, although the state could also be described in those terms. I mean the series.

Orchid Beach (1998)

Novel by Stuart Woods

GOOD COP/BAD COP

There are bad cops, and then there are bad neighborhoods. Put the two together, as bestselling author Stuart Woods does in this, the first of his Orchid series, and you've got some serious trouble. That's what ex-army major Holly Barker learns before she even gets her feet wet in her new assignment as chief of police in the fictional Orchid Beach, located on a barrier island off the east coast of Florida, not far south of the real-life Sebastian Inlet.

Gated communities are a common feature of Florida real estate. Whether they are HOAs (homeowner associations—only the home or condo is owned by the homeowner) or PUDs (planned urban developments—home, land and common areas are owned by homeowners), visitors and service people often must punch in a code or show an ID to a guard to enter. In the latter case, at least, they do so only at the pleasure of the homeowners, who incidentally get to simply insert a card or display a medallion to enter themselves. Benefits of these developments include amenities from tennis courts, golf courses and spas to clubhouse entertainment, a sense of community and privacy, reduced traffic and well-maintained grounds, as well as, of course, enhanced security—sometimes lots of it.

These communities vary greatly in terms of size and price. Supposedly the most expensive in the country, according to Forbes, is the Royal Palm Yacht and Country Club in Boca Raton, with recent listings in the $4 million to $40 million range. Fancy, yes. But even that is likely not quite as fancy as

Orchid Beach's Palmetto Gardens, the 1,500-acre home to two hundred or so families, featuring its own 6,000-foot airfield and marina (and a private port of entry staffed by customs officials imported from the mainland), and a 10-foot-high triple fence, with razor wire and electricity to help keep locals out. And did I mention the super-fancy communications center and the fact that most of the employees, even the restaurant staff, carry guns?

Why the overkill in security? (Pun intended.) That's what Holly, her new lawyer boyfriend, her ex-military dad and eventually more than a few FBI agents want to know. And how is it linked to the murders of the police chief who hired her and his best friend? And which of the cops was this deceased policeman warning her about when he told her that he had a mole in his organization?

By the way, Woods was no stranger to crime fiction when he turned his attention to Florida. The author of about one hundred books, he eventually set six novels in Orchid Beach. Unlike much other Florida fiction, his novels don't pay a huge amount of attention to the state's flora and fauna, weather or, for that matter, lifestyle. But you will learn that the next time you show your driver's license to a security guard in one of those gated communities, you might want to check his nametag. Just maybe think twice before you look him square in the eyes.

FUN FACT ABOUT *ORCHID BEACH*

In his acknowledgments, Woods coyly thanks the residents of a Florida town that, he notes, resembles Orchid Beach in some ways. But he never says which town this is. It could be somewhere on the uber-wealthy Orchid Island, which really does lie south of Sebastian Inlet and is home to a billionaire or two.

The Palm Beach Story (1942)

Film Directed by Preston Sturges; Starring Claudette Colbert, Joel McCrea, Mary Astor and Rudy Vallee

TWINS IN PARADISE

In the opening frames of the screwball Preston Sturges comedy *The Palm Beach Story*, a pretty New Yorker ties up a young woman who is identical to her and locks her in a closet. She then changes into a wedding gown to meet the woman's husband-to-be at the altar. It turns out that both the bride and groom have done the same thing: stolen their twin siblings' fiancés. But what does it all have to do with Palm Beach?

Palm Beach is a stand-in for a certain kind of wealth and privilege that neither Gerry, the bride, nor Tom, the groom, could ever hope to earn on their own merits. So desperate are they to turn around their fortunes after five years of what appears to be a happy, if penniless, marriage, that Gerry devises a scheme Tom never quite buys into: they will divorce, she will marry rich, and she will help support Tom's work.

The plot is silly. The dialogue isn't much better. But fine performances and Sturges's madcap, whirlwind style keep it all floating at least as well as the magnificent yacht owned by the world's third-richest man, on which he and Gerry sail to Florida. All works out more or less okay in the end, unless we think too hard about the words on the final title card: They lived happily ever after…or did they?

If Sturges is asking his audience what is more important, ultimately, love or money, *The Palm Beach Story* begs the question. At the end of its eighty-eight-minute running time, the movie gives the leads—and their twins—both. It takes a certain kind of humor to appreciate this movie and a certain kind of cynicism to root for its ethically challenged heroes. As for Palm Beach, we are left with the impression that it's good hunting grounds for wayward millionaires, but, unlike New York, say, it's not much else. Classic movie or not, the Florida Council of Tourism is unlikely to recommend it anytime soon.

NOT ALWAYS FUN FACTS ABOUT
THE PALM BEACH STORY

Carole Lombard was set to play the role of Gerry in the movie, but after her tragic death in a plane crash in January 1942, Claudette Colbert clinched the role. Also, the title of the movie was originally "Is Marriage Necessary?" But the production code of the time considered it too racy. In addition, the cat and mouse cartoon characters Tom and Jerry were created just two years before the movie was made. Coincidence? Hardly. Just a clever idea.

Palm Royale (2024)

TV Series Created by Abe Sylvia; Based on *Mr. and Mrs. American Pie*, by Juliet McDaniel; Starring Kristin Wiig, Ricky Martin, Josh Lucas, Leslie Bibb, Allison Janney and Laura Dern, with Bruce Dern and Carol Burnett

ROYALE PAIN

Antiheroes are a staple of good fiction. It can be a tricky balancing act for viewers to hope that a slimeball gets the woman of his dreams, but a well-crafted story can help us see the character's humanity even if we don't wish to sit and have a beer with him. In this ten-part series, however, which is based on the 2018 beach read *Mr. and Mrs. American Pie*, by Juliet McDaniel, it's often hard to root for anyone. Unless you count Norma, played by the veteran actress Carol Burnett, who, at age ninety-one, can get a laugh even while playing someone who is robbed while in a coma. (Don't worry. She has lines later, and no, they're not just on her face.)

The series creators have moved the story's action from Scottsdale, Arizona, to the even more snooty Palm Beach, Florida. The year is still 1969, at the cusp of the second wave of feminism, embodied mainly by Laura Dern as a long-haired, floppy-hatted activist. Why the move? Society women in Palm Beach then, as now, are an easy target—and their native habitat is arguably more colorful than anywhere in Arizona. All those long cars and pastel colors, sprayed-on hairdos and displays of competitive volunteering are always good for a laugh. The thing is, when the series casts the wealthy, hypocritical snobs against an ex-beauty queen, scam artist, ultimate society wannabe from Tallahassee (Wiig), it can be hard to know which way to empathize.

Tony Palm Beach is the setting for *Palm Royale*. *Wikimedia Commons.*

This, naturally, is the point. *Palm Royale* is a satire of goings-on at the "most exclusive club in the world," which refers not only to the fictional location but also to the bona fide, high society set. That group is crystallized in Maxine's bible: the (still publishing) *Shiny Sheet*, a weekly compendium of the goings-on (think balls and galas) among the local rich and famous. The periodical has always been printed on high-end, glossy paper, so it won't leak newsprint on its high-end readers' fancy linens. Officially known as the *Daily Lake Worth News*, it debuted in 1897, and is now sold as the *Palm Beach Daily News*. Different name, different editors, same society.

Is *Palm Royale* an arrow pointed at the heart of the 1 percent? Does it remind us of how feminism matters? It's mostly too silly for that. Still, when the desperate Maxine pounds on the door of a ladies' room stall where a member of the elite stands weeping and screams, "Let me in!" maybe we can relate, just a little bit.

It's not quite *Mad Men*—although the opening credits are a bit reminiscent of that earlier series set in the 1960s in New York. Think of it as "Madcap Women."

The Paperboy (1995)

Novel by Pete Dexter

The Paperboy (2012)

Film Directed by Lee Daniels. Starring
Matthew McConaughey, Nicole Kidman, John Cusack
and Zac Efron

NORTH FLORIDA IS THE SOUTH

Here's a well-known fact about Florida: the farther north you go, the more southern it is. After all, the state borders Alabama and Georgia. Northerners and Spanish speakers tend to settle in southeast Florida, while midwesterners often opt for the Gulf Coast. The north and center of the state is mainly populated by people whose families have lived in this southern state for generations, the proverbial "Crackers." *The Paperboy* centers on these southerners. They remind us that Florida is as far south as you can get while still living in the continental United States.

The story, set in 1969, centers on a mean-as-a-snake sheriff in fictional Moat County who is found gutted like an alligator. That is to say, dead. Suspicion falls on one Hillary Van Wetter, an alligator hunter with a record who lives in the swamps and is swiftly consigned to death row. Enter Ward Jansen, a hotshot *Miami Times* investigative reporter who grew up not far from both the prison and Van Wetter's home place. He and his sidekick believe Van Wetter's sentence is a miscarriage of justice, and along with a sexpot from Alabama who has fallen in love with the prisoner, he must work to prove Van Wetter's innocence. His kid brother, meanwhile, falls for the woman—hard. And there is so much more. Racism, both casual and not so much. A jellyfish sting (watch the movie for a memorable scene involving the cure). Homosexual S&M. A young man's coming of age. Dirty tricks journalism. And plenty of murder.

The movie is narrated by the Black maid Anita, who is its heart, soul and moral center. (Considering the other characters, this is not much of a challenge.) Sadly, the Grammy-winning R&B star Macy Gray, who plays her, does not sing. But she reminds us—both verbally, when she reprimands the young man for using a racial slur, and silently, when she is dressed to leave the house but is ordered to first clean up a family member's mess—that despite the fact that the film was shot in Louisiana, we are in the Deep South of northern Florida.

FUN FACT ABOUT *THE PAPERBOY*

There really is a *Miami Times*. It's South Florida's oldest and largest Black newspaper, founded in 1923.

The Perez Family (1990)

Novel by Christine Bell

The Perez Family (1995)

Film Directed by Mira Nair; Starring Marisa Tomei, Alfred Molina, Anjelica Huston and Chazz Palminteri

THE NEW AMERICAN DREAM

They were called the Marielitos. With a dream of freedom, they came from Havana on a ninety-mile boat ride to Key West, and then they traveled on to Miami in what was known as the Mariel Boatlift, or *Exodo del Mariel*, for the harbor west of Havana from which they set sail. Some of them were criminals and some political prisoners, but most simply wanted a new life. And many of them were named Perez.

The Perez Family is the story of one of these immigrants, Juan Raul Perez, an aristocrat who was jailed twenty years earlier for burning his sugarcane fields in protest of the government. It also features a young sex worker named Dottie Perez, who wants only to ply her trade with John Wayne. (Because Elvis, as everyone knows, is dead.) This is the story of not one but several Perez families, who, through government

Mariel Boatlift refugees arrive in Key West, just like the characters in *The Perez Family*. *State Archives of Florida*.

fiat, administrative error, truth-bending and, finally, true love, intertwine their lives in order to thrive in the new world. Because in those days, at least, families found sponsors easier than singles.

The colorful and music-filled movie, with a marginal character played by the great Cuban diva Celia Cruz, recreates some of the chaos of the factual downtown Miami Orange Bowl stadium's temporary housing, the heartbreak of missing a longed-for family reunion and the promise that the United States held for many of the people who came here. It, like the book, is a comedy, with elements of real heart. Tomei's highly energetic performance includes a breakdown at the news that her hero John Wayne died before he could enjoy her services in a Hollywood she believes is only a scant few dozen miles away from Miami. (Wrong Hollywood, amiga.)

The Perez Family is a story of hope among decent people who just want to exploit loopholes in the system like anyone else in order to survive. It is a testament to what the United States still means for many refugees: an oasis of opportunity. Above all, it is a love story of men and women, of family, of country and of freedom. It includes a lush Coral Gables in Miami-Dade County, an awe-inspiring banyan tree and a time in history when Miami represented the end of one road and the beginning of the next.

FUN FACTS ABOUT *THE PEREZ FAMILY*

Christine Bell has written that, for her, each story is based on some phrase or image that won't let go. In the case of *Perez*, it was an image of a couple, seen from behind, walking up to order a café Cubano on a Miami street corner. She is joyful in a polka dot dress; he is ill at ease in shoes that don't fit. Also, controversy brewed around South Florida with the principal casting of the movie. You may be able to guess by their last names that Tomei, Huston and Palminteri were decidedly not Cuban.

Recessional (1994)

Novel by James Michener

NOT YOUR GREAT-GRANDFATHER'S NURSING HOME

In his later years, the mega-selling, Pulitzer Prize–winning author of *Tales of the South Pacific* (wartime reminiscences, some of which informed the classic musical and film *South Pacific*), *The Source* (ancient to modern civilizations in Israel), *Hawaii*, *Poland*, *Texas* and dozens of other works turned his gaze to a fictional senior living residence on the west coast of Florida. *Recessional* is neither James Michener's most successful nor most important book, and at 468 pages in paperback, it isn't even one of his longest. But it was one of his most timely—for its time.

Published in 1994, *Recessional*, which, like life, is divided into "Arrivals," "Explorations" and "Departures," is ostensibly the story of Andy Zorn, a youngish, unfairly defamed Chicago obstetrician who starts a new career as the director of an ailing Tampa retirement home. He goes on to save the life of a beautiful young traffic accident victim, with whom he eventually falls in love. He turns around the financial fortunes of the senior residence facility and, in the process, meets and assists the people who live there. And everyone, except for some of the retirees who succumb to disease and old age, lives happily ever after.

In fact, the book—the title of which refers to a piece of music played as people file out of a religious service—is as much about the foundations of a land and culture as *The Source* was. This time, Michener's milieu was relatively uncharted territory for the early 1990s: the senior living industry. Up to then, elders who couldn't or didn't choose to live completely on their own usually

Pulitzer Prize winner James Michener turned his attention to senior living in *Recessional*. *Wikimedia Commons*.

resided either with family or, if the situation were dire enough, in sterile, hospital-like nursing homes, in which they often shared a room with a stranger. But by the 1990s, thanks in part to medical advances and the aging of baby boomers, the oldest of whom turned fifty in 1996, canny developers and healthcare administrators had recognized the need for a "third way" to age. Enter independent living communities, with strict age restrictions (usually fifty-five and older) and shared entertainment, dining, sports, transportation and other amenities. Additional options, such as assisted living and skilled nursing care, are available at communities for those with more limited abilities.

Zorn's new home, The Palms, mostly exhibits the summer camp aspect of such living arrangements: the way seniors make new friends, complain about the food, take risks (including building and flying their own plane) and debate the matters of the day. It is home to a former ambassador, a university president and all manner of distinguished elders, but it also makes room for some who are down on their luck. It is also situated in the midst of some lovely natural landscape, home to egrets and all manner of other subtropical flora and fauna. And to round out the picture, there is death, including death by suicide; severe dementia; trouble with last requests; and even a bit of foul play.

Today, the world that Michener created in minute detail is not so unusual. Stop the presses: a man in his nineties can still contribute to society! A couple who has been married for seventy years is still in love! But when it came out, *Recessional* covered territory that was nearly as thrilling as the world its author chronicled in his book *Space*. Old age. The final frontier. Not a bad place to visit or, at least in Florida, live in. Today, 8.6 million Florida residents are aged fifty and older, making up about 40 percent of the population. About half of those are sixty-five and older. And many of them are doing just fine.

FUN FACT ABOUT JAMES MICHENER

Although Michener spent much of his later life in Texas, his final, unfinished book, *Matecumbe*, also takes place in Florida, this time at a real resort in the Keys.

A River in Flood and Other Florida Stories (1998)

Stories by Marjory Stoneman Douglas;
Edited by Kevin M. McCarthy

OLD FLORIDA

Around these parts, she is an icon. In fact, Marjory Stoneman Douglas (eponym of the tragically attacked Parkland high school) is such a part of twentieth-century Florida history and lore that many people are shocked to learn that, like the majority of us, she did not hail from the state. Born in 1890 in Minneapolis and raised mostly in Massachusetts, Douglas moved to Florida as a young woman and spent the last 29 of her 108 years—you read that right—doing what many would say she was born for: working to restore the unique and spectacular ecosystem of the Everglades. Best known for her masterpiece *The Everglades: River of Grass* (1947), the grande dame of the Everglades, as she was known, began her writing career with the *Miami Herald* (her father was its first publisher, when it was circulated under a different name). And she published elsewhere not only over one hundred short stories, nine of which were previously collected, but also a few novels.

The stories in this collection are centered on the great lady's South Florida stomping grounds, from Cocolobo Key—a nickname for Adams Key—in the vicinity of Key Largo, to Miami and Palm Beach. They were all published in the *Saturday Evening Post* between 1925 and 1935. Douglas set her tales, most of which present in one way or another the machinations of superficial high society types and those who aspire to be so, among lush descriptions of the rich landscape of her adopted home, including the Everglades, which, by

A River in Flood and Other Florida Stories showcases Everglades activist Marjory Stoneman Douglas's skill as a writer of fiction. *Wikimedia Commons.*

the 1920s, were already well drained, much to her disgust. She folded into her stories characters such as Mr. Watkins, an easily spotted stand-in for the brilliant real-life botanist David Fairchild, who, she claimed, first introduced her to the issue of the Everglades and whose Fairchild Tropical Botanic Garden still delights visitors to Miami. Some of Douglas's stories also echo the pirate legacy of the area around the Florida Keys, while another makes mention of the liquor smuggling taking place in the vicinity during Prohibition. There is also an oblique reference to the tragically damaging Great Miami Hurricane of 1926, the aftermath of which caused Douglas to campaign for increased awareness of the inadequacies in construction regulations in the area. We also learn about the lawlessness of places like Flamingo, once the mainland's southernmost town; polo, a sport so popular in South Florida that, for the past twenty years, the USPA National Polo Center has been located in Wellington, near Palm Beach; as well as the Gulf Stream, an ocean current that flows northward up the East Coast until it makes a right turn for Europe and has long wrought havoc for mariners.

In short, Douglas gives readers a glimpse into Florida's past, good and bad, with an emphasis on outsiders, like she once was, finding their way by either jumping into Florida with both feet or bringing some of their prejudices and preferences from the North down with them—or, like the author herself, both.

Road House (2024)

Film Directed by Doug Liman. Starring Jake Gyllenhaal, Conor McGregor, Daniela Melchior, Billy Magnussen and Jessica Williams

FIGHT CLUB NIGHT CLUB

Why would anyone decide to remake a thirty-five-year-old cult classic with a beloved deceased lead? The 1989 original *Road House,* starring the late heartthrob Patrick Swayze and directed by Rowdy Herrington, made nearly $62 million in box office receipts and still stirs the souls of bar fighters everywhere on streaming services. Who, you might ask, was clamoring for "Road House Redux"?

More than one person, apparently. Back in 2015, a remake deal was in the works, but it eventually fell apart. But by 2024, the film materialized on Amazon Prime Video. The action was relocated from a biker bar in Jasper, Missouri, to a similar establishment in the fictional Glass Key, which is supposedly south of Marathon Key and a good hike north of Key West. This partly explains why someone gave it another go. With the opportunity to set the story in the beautiful, sun-striped Florida Keys, why the heck not?

The bones of the stories, of course, are the same. The owner of a bad-news bar recruits a down-on-his-luck bouncer whose brief to clean up Dodge includes taking care of an evil businessman with an axe to grind. Like Swayze's character, Gyllenhaal's Dalton is tormented by a dark secret: he accidentally killed a man with his fists. Yes, this is a fighter with his heart in the right place. In the updated version, he even takes his victims to the hospital, where he meets the woman doctor of his dreams. There are more differences between the two. First off, at a time when stars regularly cross genres, we see a real-life fighting legend or two, mainly in the person of Ultimate Fighting Champion Conor McGregor. And two female roles have been added: one of the bar owner and the other a child. What's more, Elwood Dalton doesn't start out as a bouncer. He is a UFC ex-middleweight who is so famous that he only has to show up to scare off all the bar fight challengers and take home the prize money—which doesn't stop him from attempting suicide by train at the beginning of the movie.

You might say that Glass Key saves Dalton, and Dalton saves Glass Key. All under a pristine sky. Why would anyone want to stay in Missouri?

FUN FACTS ABOUT *ROAD HOUSE*

One fight scene with Gyllenhaal was filmed during an intermission following the weigh-in for an actual UFC fight in Las Vegas. His opponent: UFC star Jay Hieron. Also, in the aborted 2015 version, the lead role was to be given to mixed martial arts fighter Ronda Rousey.

Scarface (1983)

Film Directed by Brian De Palma; Starring Al Pacino, Steven Bauer and Michelle Pfeiffer

WHEN CRIME PAYS

What is the most impressive thing about the 1983 cult classic *Scarface*? Maybe it's the copious amounts of blood, profanity, drug use and violence. (Think dismemberment via chainsaw, for starters.) Or Al Pacino's over-the-top performance as a greedy Cuban drug lord. Then there's the extraordinarily lavish lifestyle of the cocaine smugglers.

The original *Scarface* from 1932 was based on a 1930 pulp fiction novel by a young Maurice R. Coons, better known as Armitage Trail (and a host of other pseudonyms), who died, incidentally, at the age of twenty-eight of heart failure the year the book came out. In the original, as in the earlier movie, the title referred to the gangster Al Capone, who was referred to by that nickname—for reasons that are obvious to anyone who has seen a photograph of the left side of Capone's face.

The updated version was nothing if not timely. Just a few years before it came out, the Cuban economy had tanked to such a low point that 10,000 residents stormed the Peruvian Embassy in Havana to request asylum. Cuban president Fidel Castro announced that anyone who wanted to leave the communist nation could do so, and he particularly encouraged those the state declared undesirable. It is estimated that out of 125,000 "Marielitos," more than 2,500 were hardened criminals. About half of the Cubans who came via the Mariel Boatlift, as the program was called, remained in the Miami area, and these immigrants changed the economy, politics and flavor of the area forever.

The 1983 version of the gangster is a Marielito named Tony Montana, an ex-con who finds himself, like so many others, in a makeshift refugee camp. Because Tony and three homeboys have helped out a Miami drug kingpin by murdering a former Cuban general, they receive green cards and, with them, their freedom. The four go on to work for the kingpin, only to see one of them quickly murdered, for which the remaining three exact revenge. What follows is dizzying. The drug lord's gorgeous wife and sister enter the picture; there is a monkey business trip to Bolivia; there is crossing, double-crossing, prison time, cocaine, enormous wealth and more cocaine. Needless to say, things don't end well for Tony.

As for Miami, its 1980 infusion of Latin/Caribbean culture is evident in its music, food, media and more. *Scarface* may celebrate the worst of the newcomers, but it can't help reminding Miamians of some of the best.

NOT-ALWAYS-FUN FACTS ABOUT *SCARFACE*

It was Al Pacino who saw the 1932 movie and called his manager about creating the remake. Also, screenwriter Oliver Stone was grappling with a cocaine addiction while researching the script. Talk about research.

Shadow Country (2008)

Novel by Peter Matthiessen

THE KILLER IN THE SHADOWS

The serial killer known as Edgar J. Watson lived in and around the Ten Thousand Islands in Southwest Florida toward the end of the nineteenth and early twentieth centuries. Before his life ended in a spray of bullets courtesy of his Chokoloskee neighbors, Watson was believed to have committed at least four or five murders, including that of the notorious outlaw Belle Starr. You might argue that such a monster did not deserve to have his toxic existence novelized into a National Book Award–winner like *Shadow Country*, but there it is. If *Shadow Country* teaches us anything about life, it's that it's not really fair.

The story of Ed Watson is rather well known around these parts, particularly the details of his grisly death. Peter Matthiessen, a New Yorker who dealt with similar themes of different characters over the course of his acclaimed career, says this "new rendering of the Watson legend" took him thirty years to get right. He transformed it from a single long manuscript to three separate books based on the advice of his publisher. And now, at long last, this is what we would call the director's cut. The book deals with nothing less than obsessive American greed and lust for power: first to the detriment of the disenfranchised, especially the Natives and descendants of the enslaved, and then to nature itself. Indeed, Matthiessen's impressive list of nonfiction books, including another that earned him a National Book Award, helped establish his reputation as a naturalist of the first order.

Located at the western edge of the Everglades, the Smallwood Store to which Watson was headed and at which his murderers gathered on the day of his death, still exists at 360 Mamie Street in Chokoloskee. It opened in 1906 and has served as a museum since 1990. At its prime, the store catered to the frontier entrepreneurs like Watson who made their living at the ends of the Earth as trappers, hunters, fisherman, farmers and, yes, occasionally criminals. True, most of these people were not the kind you'd want to meet in a supermarket, much less a dark alley. But their backwoods ingenuity in the face of a country that shunned them contributed enormously to the development of the state.

FUN FACTS ABOUT *SHADOW COUNTRY*

Ed Watson's original middle name was Artemas, but he changed it to simply "J." Also, the three original books that Matthiessen reworked into one were *Killing Mr. Watson* (1990), *Lost Man's River* (1997) and *Bone by Bone* (1999).

The Shimmer (2018)

Novel by Carsten Stroud

NOTHING BUT TIME

It's easy to say *where* Stroud's supernatural thriller takes place: the French Quarter of New Orleans; Fernandina Beach/Amelia Island, Jacksonville and Saint Augustine on Florida's First Coast; and Crescent Beach, about a twenty-minute drive south of the latter city. It's the *when* that's a little more tricky. That's because *The Shimmer* is a time-travel novel—not, as Stroud explains in his author's note, the kind where what you change in the past can wreak havoc with everything that comes after. That can get really annoying and complicated. Instead, it adheres to the multiverse theory espoused by physicist Hugh Everett III. Change the past, and you may simply find yourself in a slightly altered version of the present. And who wouldn't want that?

When we first meet Florida Highway Patrol sergeant Jack Redding, he is a broken man mourning the death of his beloved wife and daughter in a Christmas Eve car accident the year before. Turns out that his grandmother was fatally injured in the same place, Matanzas Inlet Bridge in Saint Augustine, sixty years earlier. What follows is nothing short of a hellacious struggle across time and space with a mysterious woman that leaves two teenage girls and their mother dead in the present, as well as a number of gangsters and several others in the past newly dead or dead again. Or re-dead. Whatever.

The time-bending murderer, Selena D'Arcy, also known as Aurelia DiSantis, also known as Diana Bowman, is mixed up with a gaggle of gangsters from one of the mob's Five Families, many of whom, as we know, made a very comfortable life for themselves in Florida in the first half of the twentieth century. Also involved is Jack Redding's grandfather as a much younger, very much alive cop on the make. Not to mention on the take.

So, what's the shimmer? First and foremost, it's a nice title. It's also, according to Stroud, a mysterious play of the light that opens the portal to another era for certain lucky individuals. Sort of like going to the beach and losing track of time. Don't you hate when that happens?

FUN FACT ABOUT CARSTEN STROUD

Canadian writer Stroud once worked as an undercover agent.

Star Island (2010)

Novel by Carl Hiaasen

FOUR-STAR ISLAND

Star Island is neither the most famous nor the best of legendary *Miami Herald* columnist Carl Hiaasen's dozens of novels for adults and children. But it unveils an aspect of Florida that many books do not. Opening with a twenty-two-year-old pop star who has recently consumed Red Bull, vodka and hydrocodone, with a chaser of birdseed and stool softener, we are witnessing what the author dubs a routine South Beach 911 call. Big names gone amok have always been big business for the tabloids; not long before this book was written, Britney Spears had a very public meltdown, with fans and haters alike placing bets on the date of her next overdose, not to mention the outcome. Star Island is a real place, but it is also a stand-in here for our celebrity-obsessed culture that takes little girls and wrings them dry for profit.

There are thirty-three luxury homes on the man-made Star Island, which is generally considered Miami Beach's most exclusive address. Home to the likes of Shaquille O'Neal, Sly Stallone, Lenny Kravitz, Madonna, Sean "P" Diddy Combs and Gloria Estefan (the city's queen of Latin music), the island sits like a polished diamond amid Biscayne Bay. You'd be excused for thinking that due to the book's title, most of the action takes place in and around that location. But you'd be wrong. Our decadent twenty-two-year-old does not live on Star Island, although her actor boyfriend rents a house there. The category 5 hurricane that is the life of pop star Cherry Pye (née Cheryl Gail Bunterman) takes place in clubs, hotels, private jets and—although we don't see it here—arenas.

As in the novel of the same name, Star Island is home to Miami's uber-rich. *Wikimedia Commons.*

The plot centers on the superstar songbird Cherry Pye, who, of course, cannot sing a note; her much smarter stand-in (for when the star, who incidentally has no knowledge of her existence, is in rehab); a particularly unkempt paparazzo; Cherry's clueless, careless parents; her savvy, exasperated promoter; plus one very scary bodyguard with a weed-whacker prosthetic. And let's not forget a bizarre former governor of the state who is a sort of eco-terrorist Robin Hood. Will Cherry Pye's upcoming concert sell enough tickets? Will her unbecoming behavior poison both it and the album on which the tour is based? Will the paparazzo successfully blackmail the star and her parents? And who will get whacked by the bodyguard?

It sounds goofy, and it is. But it also implicates every one of us who has ever sneaked a peek at the *National Enquirer* (a longtime Florida employer) for dirt on a young person who never had a chance to escape the dark-as-pitch side of fame and fortune. You can laugh, or you can cry.

FUN FACT ABOUT *STAR ISLAND*

The novel's maniacal environmentalist Clinton "Skink" Tyree figures in several other Hiaasen novels as well, starting with *Double Whammy* from 1987.

Stick (1983)

Novel by Elmore Leonard

Stick (1985)

Film Directed by Burt Reynolds; Starring Burt Reynolds, Candice Bergen, Charles Durning and George Segal

STUCK

It's one of the great mysteries of life. How does a clever, well-plotted novel from one of the world's foremost comic thriller writers turn into a fairly dull, widely panned movie? Especially when it stars a smoking-hot Burt Reynolds in tight jeans at the height of his career?

By his own report, director/star Reynolds, who wanted to make the movie as soon as he read the book about a recent ex-con in Miami—"Ernest Stickley, *c'est moi*," he would have said if he'd been paraphrasing Flaubert—was satisfied with his work. Unfortunately, the studio wasn't. He was forced to do what he considered great violence to the second half of the film, causing great consternation not only for himself but also for novelist Leonard, who had served as a screenwriter. The critics were equally distressed.

The story is fairly simple. A shambling car thief, not exactly the kind of role in which you'd imagine Reynolds, is released from prison after serving seven years for armed robbery. He comes to Miami to see an old friend, with nothing more on his mind than to get a job and stay out of trouble. If he had done just that, things might have gone well for him, but there wouldn't have been much of a story. Instead, his friend involves him in a drug deal

Burt Reynolds directed and starred in *Stick*. *Wikimedia Commons.*

gone awry in the Everglades. Quick-on-the-draw Stickley, or Stick, as he is known to his friends and enemies, kills a bodyguard and comes out alive. The good friend, not so much. Things go mostly downhill from there, as Stick seeks the $5,000 in cash the friend was owed from the dealer, and the dealer and his boss want revenge for the death. In the film, a number of side plots (love interest, daughter) fill out the story in a fairly major way.

At least Florida comes out looking like Florida. Shooting on location, the locally raised Reynolds has his hero jump from a boxcar at the onset into sand, sand and more sand. When he arrives in Miami, his first sight is a cockfight. Cuban voodoo (Santería) plays a role in the book and onscreen, as do the Everglades, the world's only ecosystem of its kind. There is a fair amount of Spanish spoken. Of course, especially in Miami in the early 1980s, drugs are front and center. And let's not forget Stick's mogul boss's forty-foot yacht and trips to Key Biscayne.

Perhaps the film's most Florida element of all is the luxurious Fontainebleau Hotel, a Miami Beach landmark since 1954, which served as a home away from home for the likes of the Rat Pack—Frank Sinatra, in particular, who filmed a scene from *A Hole in the Head* there in 1959. The hotel may have had as many roles as Sinatra, including in *Scarface*, *The Bodyguard*, *The Specialist*, *The Marvelous Mrs. Maisel* and more.

The hotel did not sue the studio for ruining its career, incidentally. It didn't have to. Neither did Reynolds, although he was so traumatized by the experience that he didn't return to directing for four years.

FUN FACT ABOUT *STICK*

Albino hitman Moke was played by real-life stuntman Dar Robinson, who invented the mechanism that allowed his fatal fall from a hotel to look like he wasn't using any safety device. It worked.

Striptease (1993)

Novel by Carl Hiaasen

Striptease (1996)

Film Directed by Andrew Bergman; Starring Demi Moore, Armand Assante, Burt Reynolds and Ving Rhames

The audiences came for the sleaze factor of a Florida strip joint. They stayed—*if* they stayed, that is—for the over-the-top performances of Reynolds and Rhames. The movie *Striptease*, based on the darkly comic Hiaasen novel, has appeared on more than one "worst movie of the year, if not ever" list. Nevertheless, it made plenty of cash for its producers. For one thing, as we know by now, sex sells. For another, when an A-list actress bares 97 percent of her body for the camera, international video rentals tend to skyrocket.

Don't blame Florida for the poor reviews. In addition to its opening shot of tanned bodies on a boat and a few hot minutes on a beach, *Striptease* provides a diverse, if sometimes confusing, potpourri of East Coast geography. We have a (bumbling, crooked) congressman campaigning for reelection in the Fifth District (roughly Jacksonville to St. Augustine) who agrees to help a woman whose case has been heard in Fort Lauderdale Civil Court, three hundred miles and about ten counties away. Assante plays a Miami cop who finds a body while on vacation, and he takes over the case alone in a jurisdiction maybe one hundred miles north of his own. There's a climactic scene in the fictitious Belle Glade (sugar) Refinery in Palm Beach County. And we learn that the stripper's dastardly ex is bouncing around between Okeechobee and Deerfield (about ninety miles apart) in an attempt to conceal his whereabouts.

But what is geography when you've got biology to worry about? *Striptease* is the story of a decent FBI office worker who loses her job due to her ex-husband's criminal past and then finds out she's lost custody of her daughter because she doesn't have a job. So, she transforms herself from a mild-mannered office worker to a stripper—er, excuse us, *dancer*, as she prefers to be called. Fresh from the role of Hester Prynne in *The Scarlet Letter* the year before, Moore certainly looks and acts the part of the gorgeous *artiste* fighting tooth and nail for her child. What follows is assault, murder, blackmail, derring-do from a bouncer with a heart of gold and lots of lecherous men ogling scantily clad women, sometimes up close and personal.

Hiaasen's work usually delivers a serious message behind the hijinks, and this caper is no exception. Big Sugar, centered in and around Belle Glade, has long enjoyed enormous subsidies from the state, despite polluting the one-of-a-kind Everglades, Lake Okeechobee—the major source of water for millions of residents—and other local waterways. Corruption in government is a major culprit. As hilariously as Reynolds oversells the role of the idiot congressman, he and the sugar baron who pays him represent a festering and, by all accounts, insuperable problem for both the environment and democracy.

Maybe that's why Moore's character is such a stiff. She's the only one in the film with a young child whose future is being sold off to the highest bidder.

FUN FACTS ABOUT *STRIPTEASE*

The strikingly obvious breast implants sported by Demi Moore were eventually removed. They were reportedly replaced at a later point with, uh, more authentic-looking breasts. Also, Angela, Moore's child in the movie, is played by her real-life daughter with Bruce Willis, Rumer.

The Styx (2009)

Novel by Jonathon King

LAND GRAB

Gilded Age (late nineteenth-century) Palm Beach was, in many ways, a different place than it is today. Black workers peddled wealthy white guests in "Afromobiles," or bicycle carts; they also took on Spanish names for the pleasure of those guests in order to participate in a winter "Negro" baseball league with a team called the Cuban Giants. Standard Oil robber baron Henry Morrison Flagler's flashy Royal Poinciana and Breakers hotels were still relatively new. You could catch a dozen hefty fish in the warm, fast-flowing ocean current known as the Gulf Stream inside of an hour, including, so it was said, a four-hundred-pound blue marlin. Lynchings in the Reconstruction-era South were still common.

But then again, some things are perennial. There are still few basements in Florida due to the state's high water table. Even a century ago, natives worried about tourists ruining the island's pristine environment, although there is still decent fishing to be found. Some folks fought development with violent means, while others grabbed land with an equal show of force. And when a white man was found dead in a Black community, a Black worker was assumed responsible for the crime, despite all evidence to the contrary.

The Styx, where the fictional murder occurs, was a real place. Named for the mythical river that carries the dead to the Underworld, the Styx housed the laborers from the Deep South who built Henry Flagler's railroad line to Miami, as well as those who built and staffed the hotels that housed the well-heeled and powerful. As many as two thousand Black residents lived in the settlement in early Palm Beach, located at what is now the intersection of North County Road and Royal Poinciana Way, under the thumb of white authorities, without adequate housing or services.

Jonathon King depicts an old story of an 1894 fire, which may or may not have actually decimated the settlement, and plants a corpse among the ashes. The young daughter of Flagler's second-in-command and a New York Pinkerton guard who works for the mogul become involved both with each other and in the search for the truth of what transpired. The answer, as it turns out, is a little too close to home for their comfort.

Throughout the novel, the class distinctions—the different rules for different communities—are stark reminders of the history of slavery in the state, which had ended just a few decades before the action occurs. It's a history that still echoes. There are ghosts who still haunt.

Sunshine State (2002)

Film Directed by John Sayles; Starring Angela Bassett,
Edie Falco, Timothy Hutton, Mary Steenburgen and
Jane Alexander

MOVING ON

The indie movie veteran and author John Sayles is as much a sociologist as he is a creative. So, when he opens a movie set in Florida with a burning replica of a pirate ship, you know he's making the opening salvo of an argument about tradition and artificiality, that is, celebrating the past, real or imagined, versus the future, real or imagined. And when the flamethrower is a young Black teen on an island that used to be a slave-holding plantation, you can figure that he's making a statement about Black communities as well.

The metaphors pile up in this story of two communities. Delrona Beach is a fictional white community on a North Florida island (here, the island is called Plantation Island, although a commemorative plaque for Amelia Island, where the movie was filmed, makes an accidental appearance) that has been singled out for development against the wishes of many of its residents. The equally unhappy Black residents, meanwhile, still live in their fictional pre-segregation neighborhood of Lincoln Beach. A "new tradition" called Buccaneer Days, which is a nod to Tampa's real-life annual celebration of its pirate legacy, known as the Gasparilla Pirate Fest, plays out against the individual pain of a Black woman's return home after being thrown out for a teen pregnancy twenty-five years earlier and a white woman's dilemma about selling her family business to developers and getting the hell out of town before she "drowns." In such a setting, the developers' bribing of city

Indie director John Sayles wrote the screenplay for *Sunshine State* with stars Angela Bassett and Edie Falco in mind. *Wikimedia Commons.*

council members and hiring hometown heroes as corporate shills just add to the overall feeling of nostalgia—from the Greek for "the pain of returning home"—gone amok.

But what if there's no home to return to? What if development bulldozes over cemeteries? What if desegregation, by most accounts a good thing, was actually the catalyst for the decimation of a beloved old neighborhood? What are we to make of a man dressed in an old-fashioned military uniform hired to participate in a historical reenactment on an old fort who tells his ex-wife, "You can't live in the past"?

Sayles is the kind of storyteller who knows that good stories do not provide pat answers; they ask good questions. No, he doesn't exactly agree with the fat cat developer—played, incidentally, by comedian Alan King at his most arrogant—who extols golf courses as "controlled nature." Yet when a sixth-generation resident sees a planned residential community on her island for the first time and remarks on its beauty, we know that the filmmaker understands the tightrope walk between preservation and innovation.

There are no easy answers, Sayles tells us. Neither is there total guilt or innocence. In the end, as King's character says, developers sell dreams. It has always been so, back at least to 1916, when Irving Berlin wrote one of the songs played over the closing credits, "In Florida Among the Palms." After all, what could be bad about dreams, as long as they're not nightmares?

FUN FACT ABOUT *SUNSHINE STATE*

Filmmaker Sayles had Angela Bassett and Edie Falco in mind for the lead roles as he was writing the screenplay. He had already worked with Bassett, but only knew Falco from seeing her work.

Sunshine State (2019)

Novel by D.P. Lyle

LIFE AND DEATH IN A SMALL TOWN

You think you know people. You grow up with them, send your kids to the same schools, see them nearly every day of your life. And then it turns out they're adulterers and killers. Well, that's life in a small town.

At least it is in the fictional small town of Pine Key, nestled off the west coast of the state between Panama City and Mexico Beach, not far from Highway 98. (Which means it should not be construed as having anything to do with the real Big Pine Key in Southeast Florida.) Nothing ever happens in Pine Key, unless you count the three murders confessed to by the serial killer and former Florida State University pre-law student Billy Wayne Baker. Several years later, the town is still, understandably, grieving. After all, each of the murdered women was a beloved member of the community. You know the town. The one where everyone knows everyone. And where three people were murdered.

Sunshine State is the creation of cardiologist D.P. Lyle, who has written a couple dozen novels featuring several different detectives, in addition to assisting with a number of top TV shows. This one finds his Alabama bar owner/ex-baseball pitcher Jake Longly and his knockout girlfriend, Nicole Jamison, flying down to Florida with an odd mission handed to them by their fellow travelers Ray (Jake's dad and Nicole's boss) and Pancake (Ray's employee and Jake's childhood friend). Ray Longly is a private eye who is being paid to dispute two of the seven convictions that sent Billy Wayne to jail. Why? It's complicated. And it sure won't get the guy out of prison. But it's an interesting premise for a mystery.

What follows is an exploration of Pine Key by the four, who, as a cover, are making a documentary about the town's response to the tragedies (produced by Nicole's famous Hollywood uncle). Even the characters admit that the solution to the mystery is taken right out of an old Hitchcock classic, but there is a well-earned twist. More important is the atmosphere we soak up of a small Florida beach town with a laid-back attitude. A town with no Starbucks, a friendly baker and a restaurateur who can introduce you to everybody connected to a murder.

So often, what the rest of the world sees in the media about Florida takes place in Orlando or Miami. And yet, like anywhere else, there are still sweet little places with good people who leave their doors unlocked and know their neighbors. Who are on a first-name basis with everyone from the cops to the mayor.

Sometimes, they also commit murder.

Suspicion of Innocence (1994)

Novel by Barbara Parker

MIAMI ROYALTY

What do you get when you mix the beautiful attorney scion of an old Miami family with the tall, dark and handsome attorney grandson of Cuban refugee royalty? One of the most audacious power couples Miami has ever seen. This first installment of the late Barbara Parker's eight-volume Suspicion series, which brings together ongoing characters Gail Connor and Anthony Quintana, has everything a true Miamian could ever want to feel at home and a lot to bring newcomers up to speed. Besides the novel's brief description of what it means to be members of important local families, readers are treated to a part–Native American character named Johnny Panther, who is not overly honest about his acquisition of an ancient mask, and the usual non-human suspects that make the place come alive: a fair amount of the Spanish language; Miccosukee/Seminole history; iconic locations, such as the History/Miami Museum, Bayside, Flagler Street, Krome Avenue and the Everglades; Cuban history, including José Marti and the Bay of Pigs; Native burial mounds; invasive Brazilian pepper; and, beneath it all, a porous layer of limestone.

Then there is the plot. Gail Connor's marriage is failing. When her partly estranged, n'er-do-well sister Renee is found dead in the Everglades, the tragedy is first ruled the result of suicide, until the circumstantial evidence begins to mount up against first Gail's husband—who was involved in a "platonic affair" with Renee—and then Gail herself. While the plot stands up just fine, this mystery is rich with not only local color, but also a strong sense of the changing tide of a city.

In *Innocence*, we see the juxtaposition of old and new money, values and culture. We learn, for instance, that back in 1732, a rescue ship set sail from Cuba for the Miami River, where its Spanish captain offered to take back any willing Tequestas who wished to escape attack from another tribe. The Natives, in turn, apparently expressed their gratitude by stealing the ship's gold and taking it back into the swamp. Then, in present-day Miami, a man claiming to be descended from the extinct Tequesta shows Quintana's cousin, another grandson of a revolutionary, where that gold and precious artifacts might be in order to make a killing—which is, in another sense of the word, exactly what comes to pass.

Perhaps the only truly admirable person in the book, in fact, is Edith Newell, the history museum's director of education. All the poor woman wants is to preserve the past. After all, there is still so much of it in a city that is constantly reinventing itself.

Swamp Story (2023)

Novel by Dave Barry

SWAMPED

Yes, you can pick up absolutely any Dave Barry creation and laugh your—head off. At the time of this writing, *Swamp Story* is his latest, and it's more than memorable. Why hasn't someone out in Hollywood (California) already grabbed the movie rights to *Swamp Story*? It's a rollicking tale from the *other* brilliantly funny *Miami Herald* employee, Pulitzer Prize–winning columnist Dave Barry. True, the bestselling Barry, a national treasure equal to Carl Hiaasen, hasn't written as many novels as has his good friend. Although Barry has published dozens of books, his weapon of choice is generally goofy nonfiction. In this case, contrary to his famous tagline ("I am not making this up"), he actually *is* making it up. Although, in fact, there's enough only-in-Florida lunacy here that who knows? Maybe it *is* nonfiction!

The crazy plot of *Swamp Story* hinges on an actual Florida legend. Apparently, a Confederate paymaster buried something like $1 million, $200,000 in gold and the rest in paper "at a point in the Everglades at a junction of two creeks, where the land rises like a camel's back." Supposedly, the money can be unearthed in the western "hump." The reason he buried it? It was clear that the end of the Civil War, and thus the Confederacy, was in sight, and he was—again, according to legend—pursued by Union troops.

Who doesn't love a legend involving gold in the Everglades in the vicinity of a Seminole reservation? Our heroine, the drop-dead gorgeous Jesse, stumbles across the treasure quite by accident on a timeout from her equally gorgeous but air-headed, narcissistic husband, Slater. We first meet Slater when he attempts to capture on video, rather than destroy, the fifteen-foot python menacing Jesse and their baby. The video is for his latest money-making scheme: a reality show to be called *Glades Man*.

Barry magically ties together (1) some very bad guys who are after Jesse and the gold, with (2) a plan to save the Bortle Brothers Bait and Beer convenience store that involves another questionable belief, this one supposedly transplanted from up north involving a "melon monster," sort of like the "real" mythical swamp ape of Florida fame, (3) a nefarious state official who is hosting the Florida python challenge (no, he is not making that up—it's an annual ten-day contest with cash prizes to capture the most members of the invasive Burmese python) and (4) a drug kingpin and Jesse's horrible ex-boyfriend/lawyer. Picture plenty of airboat rides, a 250-pound wild hog, a four-year-old's insanely expensive birthday party gone berserk and masses of TikTok fans—and you've got an idea. Movie material, am I right?

It's all a riot until you realize that Slater, who keeps erroneously calling his series-to-be *Glades Guy*, has no clue what it means to be a real Gladesman, those moonshiners and plume- and alligator-hunters of an earlier era—or that most of the kids who make the melon monster gag go viral have no connection to the mangroves, mahogany or any other parts of the world-famous swamp that development has steadily poisoned.

No wonder Barry dedicated the book to Florida, which he correctly notes may be flawed but is never boring.

FUN FACT ABOUT *SWAMP STORY*

A man in this book yells, "Stella!" This is a reference to the famous Marlon Brando line in the equally famous Elia Kazan movie (and Tennessee Williams play) *A Streetcar Named Desire* (which makes it really funny).

Swamplandia! (2011)

Novel by Karen Russell

HUCK FINN ON THE CALOOSAHATCHEE

OK, so this astonishing debut novel is not a literal retelling of Mark Twain's classic tale. But there is a long, meandering journey on a skiff down a river, during which a young child is schooled in the ways of the world—for better and for much, much worse—by a grown man who is not, shall we say, of her kind. Russell's riveting coming-of-age story of a family's near-disintegration following the death of the wife and mother takes place in the Ten Thousand Islands, an area off the southwest coast of the state replete with mangroves, alligators, swamps, buzzards and mosquitoes—lots of mosquitoes. It is, at once, a paradise and a kind of hell on Earth. Sort of like childhood.

Speaking of hell, all three of the heirs of Hilola and "Chief" Sam Bigtree go off separately in search of the Underworld once their parents either die (their mother, from cancer) or decamp (their father, because the family tourist attraction has been edged out by a more commercial competitor). The story, about love and grief not only for family but also for nature, blends the real (the short-sighted failures of the U.S. Army Corps of Engineers in Florida during the Labor Day Hurricane of 1935) with the unreal ("fakelore" about a murdered ex-slave named Mama Weeds, the town of Loomis, attractions called Swamplandia! and World of Darkness) to create an altogether believable and stunning conflict of man against nature. The Underworld also leads to perhaps the novel's only out-and-out joke: Kiwi Bigtree, the genius son of the family, notes that the presence of single-ply toilet paper in World of Darkness means that he really *is* in hell.

Before we've finished our sojourn in the swamp, we've come to understand an observation at the heart of this tale: that one cannot be a good student of history without sufficiently learning to mourn. Yes, *Swamplandia!* features alligator wrestling, child and elder abuse and rape. Suffice it to say, it is not an easy read. But the trip through the human heart, through childhood and family feeling, is worth the discomfort. At the same time, we come to appreciate the glorious landscape of a part of Florida that may not be around forever—neither, as the book reminds us, will its residents.

FUN FACT ABOUT *SWAMPLANDIA!*

Author Karen Russell won the so-called Genius Award for exceptional creativity from the MacArthur Foundation at the age of thirty-three. Also, *Swamplandia!* was nominated for a Pulitzer Prize in a year when no nominee received enough votes for the prize to be awarded.

Their Eyes Were Watching God (1937)

Novel by Zora Neale Hurston

TELLING THE BLACK FLORIDA STORY

Their Eyes Were Watching God was by no means an instant success among the members of the Harlem Renaissance, the Black cultural and intellectual movement born in New York City in 1925 and continued into the 1930s. In fact, many of the Black movers and shakers of the time, like Richard Wright and W.E.B. DuBois, widely reviled its anthropologist author, Zora Neale Hurston. Not until the 1970s did reviewers, readers and university literature departments truly embrace both her and her writing. Today, Hurston and her books celebrating old Black Florida are themselves celebrated for exactly the reasons they were once lambasted. They told it like it was.

Their Eyes is the story of Janie Crawford, an intelligent and energetic woman who endures childhood poverty, three difficult husbands and, in a stunning climax, a "monstropolous" hurricane with two-hundred-mile-per-hour winds to find a kind of freedom and selfhood virtually unknown to most women of her milieu. Most of the characters speak in a Southern Black dialect, anathema to the proponents of the "New Negro" in Manhattan but very much a reflection of the speech patterns of the sharecroppers who populated the area around Lake Okeechobee and Central Florida at the time. Characters have names like "Motorboat," "Muck-Boy" and "Tea Cake." In demonstrating the rampant sexism, abuse and alcoholism, lack of good jobs or education and general misery of the area, Hurston engaged in the fictional equivalent of "participant observation," the anthropological

Zora Neale Hurston did fieldwork in Florida as an anthropologist. *Library of Congress.*

technique of deeply engaging with one's informants. Unlike her contemporary Margaret Mead, however, she chose, both in her scientific work and in her fiction, to study the people she knew best: those she had grown up among in rural Florida. And for her work, the brilliant, outspoken and flamboyant Hurston is widely considered the foremost authority on Black folklore in her lifetime.

In 1889, the weekly newspaper of Eatonville, the novel's fictionalized setting of the town—thirty minutes from today's Disney World—in which Hurston grew up, printed the following: "Colored People of the United States: Solve the great race problem by securing a home in Eatonville, Florida, a Negro city governed by Negroes." Hurston actually wrote the book in nearby Belle Glade, an agricultural city where she studied the Black laborers in the "muck," the sticky, swampy earth that, along with mosquitoes and storms, plagued the migrant workers to no end.

She was a Columbia University–educated professional, but she refused to disavow the old in order to shepherd in the new. *Their Eyes Were Watching God* bridges the gap between the two worlds.

FUN FACTS ABOUT
THEIR EYES WERE WATCHING GOD

The Colorado-based indie band the Samples recorded a song called "Eatonville" on their fourth album, after band member Andy Sheldon read the book. Also, Hurston was great friends with fellow Floridian Marjorie Kinnan Rawlings (although neither was a native).

To Have and Have Not (1937)

Novel by Ernest Hemingway

CAPTAIN MORGAN'S RUN

Surprised that this novel is actually set in Florida during the Depression and not, say, in Vichy France during World War II? That's because the classic 1944 Howard Hawks vehicle for Humphrey Bogart and Lauren Bacall changed the setting and period, not to mention the politics, of the original. Three more movie adaptations followed with varying titles, placing the action between Southern California and the Persian Gulf. But while the story may depict a universal struggle, it's actually pure Florida—with neighboring Cuba playing an important role.

Hemingway knew whereof he wrote. The Idaho native and Nobel Prize–winning writer may have been born and died elsewhere, but Key West claims him for its own, with the author's home in the 1930s at 907 Whitehead Street still the area's most popular tourist attraction. And annual Hemingway look-a-like contests fill the island city with bearded men. He wrote this novel while living there.

While the novel *To Have and Have Not* is set in Florida, the movie takes place in France. *Wikimedia Commons*.

Not only is the Depression destroying local lives and livelihoods during the period of the novel, but a Cuban revolution is also taking place. It wasn't Castro's revolution, however. Gerardo Machado, the island nation's first dictator, was ousted in 1933 by none other than Fulgencio Batista, who himself became the dictatorial target of Castro and Che Guevera decades later.

If you can't keep up with the politics, that's OK. All you need to know is that the combination of Cuban revolutionaries and hard economic times are making life difficult for retired policeman and current fishing boat captain Harry Morgan. Getting stiffed by a client at the book's opening sets off his spiral from hardworking small businessman to cynic, smuggler and murderer. Even the love of a good woman can't save him or his pals at the bottom of the heap. Interestingly enough, the "haves" at the top aren't doing all that well, either, what with their marital and drinking problems. But at least they have enough food and housing, as opposed to the book's "have nots."

As in most any Hemingway novel, the book's plot is deceptively simple, and the writing is spare. Yet it is rich not only in human and political insight but also in fishing detail. Today, anglers from all over the world come to the Keys for redfish, trout, permit, pompano, tarpon, mahi mahi and more. Keys fishing is big business, both for real-life tourist guides and for commercial fishermen working in the seafood industry.

As for the inextricable link with Cuba in the novel, Key West is just about ninety miles north of the island country. Harry Morgan could have done that distance with his eyes closed.

FUN FACT ABOUT *TO HAVE AND HAVE NOT*

The reason the setting was switched from the United States and Cuba in the 1930s to France and Martinique in 1940 was due to the American "Good Neighbor policy" of nonintervention into the affairs of Latin American countries implemented by the administration of Franklin D. Roosevelt.

Ulee's Gold (1997)

Film Directed by Victor Nuñez; Starring Peter Fonda,
Patricia Richardson, Christine Dunford, Tom Wood
and Jessica Biel

THERE'S GOLD IN THEM THAR HIVES

Suffice it to say, the Florida honey industry is not what it used to be.
Modernization has changed it like it has any other agricultural pursuit here.
Nevertheless, the Lanier family, a member of whom served as a consultant
for *Ulee's Gold*, is still producing rare tupelo honey (cue Van Morrison, who
sings his classic song over the end credits) by hand from the white ogeechee
tupelo tree, as it has since the late 1800s. The movie is set in Wewahitchka, a
very apt Native expression meaning "water eyes." Wewa, as it's also called, is
a tiny city along the Chipola River in the Florida Panhandle, known for bass
fishing, the spectacular Dead Lakes and, yes, the manufacture of precious
high-fructose, only-in-Florida honey.

The labor-intensive craft of tupelo honey production is front and center in
Nuñez's movie, which follows the slow and steady emotional rehabilitation
of Ulee Jackson, who is caring for his two granddaughters while their
father serves time for robbery and their mother is temporarily MIA. Drug
addiction in the form of aftereffects from the "date rape" drug Rohypnol
and memories of the Vietnam War, as well as crime, state prison, guns and
violence, all play out against the backdrop of the idyllic landscape, with its
cypress knees, waterways and magnificent greenery. We learn that Ulee's lack
of affection is due at least in part to the recent death of his wife. To add to
his problems, there's the impossible workload for a man of a certain age, an

The hard work that goes into making Florida honey is on full display in *Ulee's Gold*. *Wikimedia Commons*.

aversion to asking for assistance from non–family members, lingering pain from the fact that he was the only one from his unit to return from the war, and the agony of having watched his son descend into a lifestyle that landed him in the state prison system. Through it all, the only constant is the hard life that this hard man has inherited from his ancestors. When the girls and his finally returned daughter-in-law pitch in to help get out the honey on a tight deadline, we catch a glimpse of what it means to be a family with a legacy like theirs.

And then there are those bees. As Ulee explains the "understanding" that he and the bees have to take care of each other, we are reminded of the opening shot: closeups of just one of him juxtaposed with those of thousands of them. Although *Ulee's Gold* is closer to a thriller than a family saga, that relationship serves as a promise of a certain kind of kinship and a certain kind of Florida industry.

Under Cover of Daylight (1987)

Novel by James W. Hall

A DEVELOPING NIGHTMARE

Developers. Can't live with 'em, can't live without 'em. But when it comes to the latter option, many native or longtime Floridians would sure love to try. Former Florida International University professor and bestselling crime novelist James W. Hall launched his sixteen-book Thorn series, about a low-key bonefish fisherman-turned-private investigator, with this love letter to a Keys locale that, in the mid-'80s, was already hovering on the knife edge between authentic and plastic.

Thorn is a morose but recently hopeful loner living in the Key Largo stilt house where he grew up, just twenty feet from a quiet, mangrove-rimmed bay. His side gig is making killer lures with names like the Flig, the Muddler, Bone Buster and Crazy Charlie for a handful of fly fishermen who show up at his dock on a regular basis. The reason for his newfound hope: a beautiful young Miamian who seems to be as attached to him as he is to her—but she looks strangely, unsettlingly, familiar. The young woman, who, with no spoiler alert required, is not quite what she seems, also takes a shine to Thorn's beloved adoptive mother Kate, an anti-development activist and boat captain with a list of local haters a mile long. What follows is grisly murder, drug smuggling, double-crossing and the revelation of both new and old secrets, during which Thorn is thrust into a role he seems to have been born for: crime solver.

Old Key West is at risk of overdevelopment in *Under Cover of Daylight*. *Wikimedia Commons*.

There are also plenty of boats and fishing, especially, in one memorable scene, for out-of-season yellowtail. On the water and off, the Keys are featured here in all their glory, and much of the plot centers on the against-all-odds fight to keep them as pristine as possible in the face of locals clamoring for jobs and one developer in particular who will stop at nothing to get his latest deal, a four-hundred-acre "small city," signed, sealed and built.

When Thorn arrives at a bar and casually asks why no one is wearing a shirt, he is reminded with an adjectival expletive that he is in the Keys. And yet, the more tourists and New York transplants who arrive, the less Keys-like the place is. It's a truism that every newcomer to Florida wants to lock the gates behind them, keeping it just the way they found it. The sad joke, of course, is that, like everywhere else, it changes every day. And the saddest people to hear that joke are those who, like Thorn, are graduates of local high schools. They may not be Natives, but they're native to the area. And they're fighting for what's been theirs all their lives—sometimes to the death.

Where the Boys Are (1960)
Novel by Glendon Swarthout

Where the Boys Are (1960)
Film Directed by Henry Levin; Starring Connie Francis, Dolores Hart, Paula Prentiss, George Hamilton, Yvette Mimieux, Jim Hutton and Frank Gorshin

Where the Boys Are (1984)
Film Directed by Hy Averback; Starring Lisa Hartman Black, Russell Todd, Lorna Luft and Wendy Schaal

SPRING BROKE

Every year, sometime around the second and third weeks of March, college students embark on a time-honored quest for fun known as spring break. For a long time, the prime destination for these intrepid souls was Fort Lauderdale Beach, and for a long time, the City of Fort Lauderdale couldn't have been happier. It is said that the tradition began as far back as 1935, with the creation of a winter break swim meet known as the Collegiate Aquatic Forum. Those students who attended began to promote the city and its beaches as a great getaway destination. The city also mailed invitations to northern colleges. As returning World War II veterans raised college enrollment and youth culture spread in the 1950s, the spring break tradition grew to the point that, by 1960, the year that *Where the Boys Are* hit theaters, Bahia Mar in Fort Lauderdale and the notorious Elbo Room Beach Bar, a neighborhood fixture since 1938, were ground zero for thousands of young adults to descend and party, swim, party, suntan—and party. Think wet T-shirt contests and drink specials. As early as 1954, city elders in "Fort Liquordale" realized they had a problem. Residents complained about the noise, garbage and traffic. Business owners complained about the petty theft, vandalism and general craziness. Cops complained about just about everything, including the mounting death toll from traffic accidents, alcohol poisoning and other scourges.

So it was that the book and original movie both reflected and fanned the flames of the commotion. The story of four coeds traveling from blizzard conditions in the Midwest to bare midriffs in the Southeast, *Boys* is about as frank a depiction of premarital sex, rape, mob mentality, mermaids in a tank and drinking to excess as moviegoers were likely to expect at the time. The movie also features a little jazz and international recording star Francis's rendition of the movie's theme song, which charted to no. 4 and became her signature hit.

At the time of this writing, incidentally, Francis is alive and fairly well at eighty-six. But what about spring break in Fort Lauderdale? The overall hooliganism reached a point in 1985, the year that 350,000 students descended on the beach and about 889 of them unwillingly visited the city jail for part of their stays, that those same city elders realized it was high time to put the kibosh on the merriment (this despite the $120 million the merrymakers added to the tax base). Thanks to the work of then-mayor Robert Dressler, who actually appeared on the popular TV show *Good Morning America* with an urgent appeal to would-be visitors, spring break began to break. The middle of State Road A1A, the main drag along the beach, was temporarily barricaded, so students could only cross from the bars to the beach at certain points. New ordinances, such as prohibitions against public drinking, overnight beach parking and hotel room overcrowding (celebrated in this movie, incidentally) were strictly enforced. No big surprise: news of the change spread, and cancellations poured in. For those who braved the restrictions, by the end of spring break 1986, more than 2,500 students were arrested. The next year, most of the kids went elsewhere, and business along the beach, predictably, never recovered.

The city elders aren't totally thrilled.

FUN FACTS ABOUT *WHERE THE BOYS ARE*

Star Dolores Hart left Hollywood at the peak of her career to become a Benedictine nun. The novel (and subsequent movie's) title came from a coed's quote in a *Time* magazine article on the subject. When asked why she made the trip to Fort Lauderdale, she replied, "This is where the boys are."

The Yearling (1938)

Novel by Marjorie Kinnan Rawlings

The Yearling (1946)

Film Directed by Clarence Leon Brown; Starring Gregory Peck, Claude Jarman Jr. and Jane Wyman

The Yearling (1994)

Film Directed by Rod Hardy; Starring Peter Strauss, Jean Smart, Philip Seymour Hoffman and Wil Horneff

COMING OF AGE IN CENTRAL FLORIDA

Well, you might have heard it here first: one of the quintessential Florida novels was, in fact, written by a Yankee. *The Yearling*, arguably the most famous fictional depiction of rural life in the state's first century, is a coming-of-age story about a child and a baby deer written by Washington, D.C., native Marjorie Kinnan Rawlings. She wasn't technically a Yankee, but her birthplace is still a long way north of the Florida border, which is mighty hard to believe when you read this novel.

Rawlings migrated to the Sunshine State with her husband, Charles, in 1928 at the age of thirty-two. The couple purchased seventy-two acres of pristine wilderness between two lakes in Central Florida in a settlement (now an unincorporated community) called Cross Creek, situated in Alachua

County, approximately twenty miles southeast of Gainesville. (The family homestead, which is also where the movie of the same name was shot, is now located within the Ocala National Forest.) Four novels, one major book prize, two award-winning feature films, a Broadway musical and a TV movie later, Rawlings, who remained in Florida until her death a quarter of a century later, certainly put little Cross Creek on the map.

The plot of the Pulitzer Prize–winning novel is simple: the yearling in question refers not only to Flag, the orphaned fawn that young Jody Baxter adopts after his father kills the animal's mother, but also Jody himself, who learns how to become a man while navigating the difficult life of a poor Central Florida farmer and hunter in the mid-nineteenth century. The book's disturbing climax underscores the harshness of the landscape, but set pieces throughout highlight the extraordinary challenges, along with small moments of solidarity and joy, that these isolated families faced. The detailed descriptions of food ways, hunting and farming techniques and the flora and fauna of the Baxters' environment are testament to the one-time journalist Rawlings's extensive research.

If you read the book, you'll learn so much about the state, you may just sound like a Florida native yourself.

FUN FACTS ABOUT *THE YEARLING*

Rawlings was sued for $100,000 for invasion of privacy by a Cross Creek friend and neighbor for her less-than-flattering depiction of the woman in some of her other writing. She won the case, but it was overturned on appeal. Although she owed only a dollar, she never wrote another book about Florida. Also, in the film, Gregory Peck played Jody's father, Penny, so nicknamed because he was a tiny man. The actor, however, reportedly stood at six foot, three inches tall.

Selected Sources

Allen, Dan. "Tarell Alvin McCraney: The Man Who Lived *Moonlight*." NBC News. October 20, 2016. www.nbcnews.com/feature/nbc-out/tarell-alvin-mccraney-man-who-lived-moonlight-n670296.

Alleyne, Rochelle. "New Link Between Defunct Southwest Florida Cult and Branch Davidians in Waco." ABC Action News. www.abcactionnews.com/news/state/new-link-between-defunct-southwest-florida-cult-and-branch-davidians-in-waco.

Amnesty International. "United States of America: Florida Reintroduces Chain Gangs." January 1996. https://www.amnesty.org/es/wp-content/uploads/2021/06/amr510021996en.pdf.

Bell, Christine. "About." www.christinesaintbell.com/about.

Bridges, C.A. "Sharks Lightning Rough Surf: The Most Dangerous Beaches in Florida, by the Numbers." *The Daytona Beach News-Journal*, March 11, 2024. www.news-journalonline.com/story/news/2024/03/11/florida-shark-bites-attacks-drownings-rank-new-smyrna-beach-panama-city-most-dangerous/72786726007/.

Butler, Deanna. "A Land Remembered by Patrick D. Smith." Florida Seminole Tourism. July 21, 2023. https://floridaseminoletourism.com/a-land-remembered-by-patrick-d-smith/.

Cohen, Howard. "How *Miami Vice* Changed TV." *Miami Herald*, September 17, 2018.

Cream. "Interview with Jeff Lindsay: Author of the *Dexter* Novels and Consultant to the Series." November 23, 2021.

Crowley, Kinsey, and Steve McQuilkin. "Florida's Next Invasive Species? A Crab-Eating Monkey Related to Deadly, Swimming Monkeys: Report." USA Today. January 14, 2024. www.usatoday.com/story/news/nation/2024/01/11/invasive-species-in-florida/72119813007/.

The Daily Gardener. "John Laroche: The Orchid Thief." https://thedailygardener.org/ota20210219/.

Doc Ford's Rum Bar & Grille. www.docfords.com.

Dunbar, Eve. "What I Learned About Love from Rereading *Their Eyes Were Watching God.*" American Masters. PBS. June 8, 2017. www.pbs.org/wnet/americanmasters/blog/learned-love-rereading-eyes-watching-god/#:~:text=Richard%20Wright%2C%20often%20considered%20Hurston's,choosing%20sensuality%20over%20social%20commentary.

Exploring Florida. "Florida's Shipwrecks and Treasures." https://fcit.usf.edu/florida/lessons/shipwrecks/shipwrecks.htm#:~:text=Explorers%20and%20settlers%20arrived%20in,shallow%20shores%2C%20and%20even%20pirates.

Ezell, Brice. "*The Palm Beach Story* and the Comedy of Patriarchy." PopMatters. February 20, 2015. https://www.popmatters.com/190610-the-palm-beach-story-and-the-comedy-of-patriarchy-2495560660.html.

Farrell, Jodi Mailander. "Loch Lomond, Pompano Beach: Most Diverse Neighborhood in Florida." Visit Florida. www.visitflorida.com/travel-ideas/articles/pompano-beach-loch-lomond-most-diverse-neighborhood-florida.

Fear, David. "*Bad Boys: Ride or Die* Isn't a Sequel, It's a Career Hail Mary." *Rolling Stone*, June 7, 2024. https://www.rollingstone.com/tv-movies/tv-movie-reviews/bad-boys-4-review-will-smith-1235029676/.

Ferrier, Aimee. "Visit the Real-Life Filming Locations of Sean Baker's *The Florida Project.*" Far Out. October 6, 2022. https://faroutmagazine.co.uk/visit-filming-locations-sean-bakers-the-florida-project/.

Flamer, Keith. "Museum Curators and Cats Ride Out Hurricane Irma in Ernest Hemingway's Historic Key West Home." *Forbes*, September 10, 2017. www.forbes.com/sites/keithflamer/2017/09/10/museum-curators-cats-ride-out-hurricane-irma-in-ernest-hemingways-historic-key-west-home/?sh=667e530115eb.

Florida Department of Corrections. "Death Row." https://fdc.myflorida.com/ci/deathrow.html.

Florida Division of Arts and Culture. "Marjorie Kinnan Rawlings: Author." https://dos.fl.gov/cultural/programs/florida-artists-hall-of-fame/marjorie-kinnan-rawlings/.

FloridaHumanities. "Patrick Smith: *A Land Remembered*." September 12, 2013. www.youtube.com/watch?v=aIrgDqZ9aIE.

Florida Keys Commercial Fishermen's Association. https://fkcfa.org/.

Florida Memory. "Ivan Tors Studios in Miami." www.floridamemory.com/items/show/232437.

———. "The Koreshan Unity." www.floridamemory.com/learn/exhibits/koreshan/.

The Florida Roundup. "Summer Reading Special: Authors Lauren Groff, Doris Kearns Goodwin and Dick Batchelor on Florida." May 24, 2024. https://www.wlrn.org/show/the-florida-roundup/2024-05-24/summer-reading-special-authors-lauren-groff-doris-kearns-goodwin-and-dick-batchelor-on-florida.

Freakanomics Radio. "A Social Activist in Prime Minister's Clothing." Episode 585. Aired April 28, 2024. https://www.npr.org/podcasts/452538045/freakonomics-radio.

Gulf County, Florida. "Wewahitchka." www.visitgulf.com/destinations/wewahitchka/.

History. "Cuban Revolution." August 9, 2023. www.history.com/topics/latin-america/cuban-revolution.

IMDb. "*Key Largo*: Trivia." www.imdb.com/title/tt0040506/trivia/.

———. "*The Palm Beach Story*: Trivia." www.imdb.com/title/tt0035169/trivia/.

Knowlton, Christopher. *Bubble in the Sun: The Florida Boom of the 1920s and How It Brought on the Great Depression*. Simon & Schuster, 2020.

The Luxury Team. "Royal Palm: Listing Report." https://royalpalmexpert.com/listing-report/Royal-Palm/2159991/?gad_source=1&gclid=EAIaIQobChMIoJK5xcHRhgMVprlaBR2ZWAUlEAAYASADEgK2uvD_BwE.

Marca. www.marca.com.

Martin, Andrew. "From Jamaican to Miamian, and All the Identities in Between." *The New York Times*, September 4, 2022. www.nytimes.com/2022/09/04/books/review/jonathan-escoffery-if-i-survive-you.html.

Maslin, Janet. "Handling a Pop Star, Cattle Prod Included." *The New York Times*, July 21, 2010. www.nytimes.com/2010/7/21/books/21book.html.

McGrath, Campbell. *Florida Poems*. New York: Ecco, 2002.

Mel Fisher's Treasures. www.melfisher.com.

Mia Aesthetics. www.miaaesthetics.com.

Miami History. "Greater Miami During World War II." https://miami-history. com/podcasts/greater-miami-during-wwii/#:~:text=The%20area%20 became%20the%20training,area%20was%20the%20war%20effort.

Mondello, Bob. "*Florida Project* Turns a Decrepit Corner of Orlando into a Cinematic Playground." *All Things Considered*. National Public Radio. Aired on October 6, 2017.

Mormino, Gary R. "The Enduring but Endangered Symbol of Florida." *Ocala Star-Banner*, April 10, 2016. www.ocala.com/story/ opinion/2016/04/10/gary-r-mormino-the-enduring-but-endangered-symbol-of-florida/31971297007.

Office of Attorney General Ashley Moody. "Records, Disclosure of Jurors' Names, Number AGO 2005-61." November 21, 2005. www. myfloridalegal.com/ag-opinions/records-disclosure-of-jurors-names#:~:text=Accordingly%2C%20consistent%20with%20the%20 decision,by%20the%20clerk%20of%20court.

The Official Website of Greater Miami and Miami Beach. "Art Deco Historic District." www.miamiandbeaches.com/l/attractions/art-deco-historic-district/2116.

OnlineSchools.org. "The Story Behind Spring Break." www.onlineschools. org/visual-academy/spring-break/.

Orlean, Susan. "Orchid Fever." *The New Yorker*, January 15, 1995. www. newyorker.com/magazine/1995/01/23/orchid-fever.

PBS. "Biography: David Koresh." www.pbs.org/wgbh/pages/frontline/ waco/davidkoresh.html#:~:text=David%20Koresh%20was%20 born%20Vernon,was%20raised%20by%20his%20grandparents.

Peters, Xander. "Citrus Crisis: As an Iconic Florida Crop Fades, Another Tree Rises." *The Christian Science Monitor*, March 2, 2023. www.csmonitor. com/Environment/2023/0302/Citrus-crisis-As-an-iconic-Florida-crop-fades-another-tree-rises#:~:text=storied%20tradition%20behind.-,The%20citrus%20industry%2C%20long%20a%20defining%20 symbol%20of%20Florida%2C%20is,Today%2C%20there%20are%20 about%202%2C000.

Pinkerton, Nick. "Interview with George Armitage." *Film Comment*, April 2, 2015.

Publishers Weekly. "*The Perez Family*." www.publishersweekly.com/9780393027983.

Radish, Christina. "Why Annette Bening Made the Jump to TV with Her New Miniseries, *Apples Never Fall*." Collider. March 15, 2024. https:// collider.com/apples-never-fall-annette-bening/.

Rainer, Peter. "Movie Review: *The Perez Family*: Saga in Need of a Themostat." *Los Angeles Times*, May 12, 1995. www.latimes.com/archives/la-xpm-1995-05-12-ca-65303-story.html.

Robbins, Ira P. *"Explaining Florida Man." Florida State University Law Revie*w 1 (2021): 49.

Rozsa, Lori. "How Florida Is Getting Its Pink Bank." *The Washington Post*, May 26, 2024.

Schiltz, James. "Time to Grow Up: The Rise and Fall of Spring Break in Fort Lauderdale." *Florida Historical Quarterly* 93, no. 2 (2014): 195–225.

SeniorLiving.org. "Florida Assisted Living Costs & Statistics." July 25, 2024. www.seniorliving.org/assisted-living/florida/.

Sepinwall, Alan, and Matt Zoller Seitz. *TV (The Book): Two Experts Pick the Greatest American Shows of All Time.* Grand Central Publishing, 2016.

Sitcoms Online. "Spinoffs & One Year Wonders." www.sitcomsonline.com/boards/showthread.php?t=313034#google_vignette.

Sneider, Jeff. "Christian Bale Eyed to Play Travis McGee in *The Deep Blue Good-by*." TheWrap. July 15, 2014. www.thewrap.com/christian-bale-eyed-to-play-travis-mcgee-in-the-deep-blue-good-by/.

———. "Leonardo DiCaprio Exits Travis McGee Movie *The Deep Blue Good-by*." TheWrap. March 4, 2014. www.thewrap.com/leonardo-dicaprio-exits-travis-mcgee-movie-deep-blue-good/.

South Florida Sun-Sentinel. "West Boynton Hits the Big Screen." September 27, 2021. www.sun-sentinel.com/2006/12/10/west-boynton-hits-the-big-screen/.

Stade, George. "Villains Have the Fun." *The New York Times*, March 6, 1983, 7:11.

Stanley, Alessandra. "The Further Adventures of Two Body Upholsterers." *The New York Times*, September 5, 2006. www.nytimes.com/2006/09/05/arts/television/05nip.html.

Stevens, Mark. "Britney Spears, Outsider Artist." *New York*, February 23, 2007. *https://nymag.com/news/intelligencer/features/28528/.*

Strange History X. "The Untold Story of Ivan Tors." January 20, 2021. www.youtube.com/watch?v=4pLMFYA1ybo.

TheDarkOrchid.com. www.thedarkorchid.com.

TreasureNet. "Confederate Gold: Sories of Other and Any Help with This One." www.treasurenet.com/threads/confederate-gold-stories-of-others-and-any-help-with-this-one.110832/.

Tupelo Honey. www.tupelohoney.com/.

TVTropes. "Film: *The Palm Beach Story*." https://tvtropes.org/pmwiki/pmwiki.php/Film/ThePalmBeachStory.

U.S. Department of Homeland Security. "Fact Sheet: Changes to Parole and Expedited Removal Policies Affecting Cuban Nationals." January 12, 2017. https://www.dhs.gov/sites/default/files/publications/DHS%20Fact%20Sheet%20FINAL.pdf.

Viglucci, Andres. "The Vice Effect: 30 Years After that Show that Changed Miami." *Miami Herald*, September 28, 2014.

The Village at Castle Pines. "The Pros and Cons of Living in a Gated Community." September 11, 2023. https://thevillagecastlepines.com/pros_and_cons_of_living_in_a_gated_community/.

Walker, Michael. "*Miami Vice* Ferrari to Be Auctioned." *The Hollywood Reporter*, August 12, 2015.

West Palm Beach. "Task Force on Racial & Ethnic Equality." https://www.wpb.org/Our-City/Office-of-Mayor-Keith-A.-James/Task-Force-on-Racial-Ethnic-Equality.

WUSF. "Prisoners in the US Are Part of a Hidden Workforce Linked to Hundreds of Popular Food Brands." January 29, 2024. https://www.wusf.org/courts-law/2024-01-29/prisoners-us-florida-hidden-workforce-linked-hundreds-popular-food-brands.

About the Author

Caren Schnur Neile, PhD, MFA, is a performance storyteller and author who taught storytelling studies at Florida Atlantic University in Boca Raton for over two decades. A former Fulbright senior specialist, Dr. Neile has presented in fourteen states and eight countries. She has published numerous articles and book chapters, as well as six books, and is the former chair of the National Storytelling Network and a cofounder of the international academic journal *Storytelling, Self, Society.* She also appears regularly on Miami public radio WLRN's *Public Storyteller* podcast, which she coproduces.

Visit us at
www.historypress.com